Stephanie's "Learn How to Draw"

Drawing Lessons with Grids

Also by Stephanie Relfe

Stephanie's "Learn How to Draw Horses" Drawing Lessons With Grids

You're Not Fat. You're Toxic.
A permanent weight loss and natural health program

Homeschool Natural Health & Biology Comprehension Curriculum Workbook, for Grades 7 - 12. A companion
to *You're Not Fat. You're Toxic*

Perfect Health with Kinesiology and Muscle Testing
DVD Training Course

Perfect Health with Kinesiology and Muscle Testing
Training Manual

Perfect Health with Kinesiology and Muscle Testing
Practitioner Manual

Stephanie's "Learn How to Draw"

Drawing Lessons with Grids

Stephanie Relfe B.Sc.

Sherrington House

Stephanie's "Learn How to Draw". Drawing Lessons with Grids™

1st Edition

Published 2015 by Sherrington House

Printed in the United States of America

Stephanie's "Learn How to Draw" Drawing Lessons with Grids™ is a trademark of Stephanie Relfe.

International Standard Book Number: 978-0-9895899-1-8

10 9 8 7 6 5 4 3 2 1   21 20 19 18 17 16 15

Stephanie's "Learn How to Draw"

Contents

Why You Can Draw

& Why this is Important

It has been estimated that less than 5% of people can draw. To many people, the process of drawing seems mysterious and somehow beyond human understanding. This is a terrible and needless situation. This is like saying that before the Industrial Revolution, most people could not read or write, and so no one can ever learn to do so. Anyone who can hold a pencil and write legibly can learn to draw well, whether they are four years old or eighty years old. You just have to teach your brain how to move a pencil in the correct direction.

This book will get you started. Don't think you can't do the exercises in this book because "you can't draw"! That's like not learning the alphabet because you can't read, or not learning to count because you can't do math!

DRAWING COMES BEFORE ART

Most people think that drawing is art, but drawing is not art, although drawing does come before art, just as counting comes before math, and the alphabet comes before reading.

There are many benefits to learning drawing, even if you do not want to go on and become an artist. I will discuss these benefits in more detail in the next pages. These benefits include:

- Increase the ability of the right brain, so that the person becomes whole- brained.

- Increase the ability to perceive and solve problems with new solutions.

- Have another means of communication through visual methods.

- Gain self-confidence because you know you can draw.

- Have a natural way to totally relax and feel blissfully happy.

DRAWING IS TO ART, AS COUNTING IS TO MATH, OR THE ALPHABET IS TO READING

There are some people who say they can't learn to draw because they say "I can't draw". That's like saying that a person can't learn to count, because they can't do math, or can't learn the alphabet because they can't read. It's back to front. Drawing is a basic skill anyone can learn. It has to be learned before a person will be a good artist.

Somehow people stopped teaching people to draw, if they ever did. Instead, the art department goes straight to "art", and only a few survive. This book will get you started with drawing.

THE FOURS STEPS TO ART ARE:

1) Line Drawing. This book will teach you that.

2) Shading.

3) Color.

4) Painting.

DRAWING GIVES YOU A FULL BRAIN

Learning to draw is important for everyone to do, not just children, because drawing exercises the right brain, generally. Unfortunately, nearly everything you learned at school exercised only the left brain, which means that most schooling is a half-brained affair.

For us to grow to our maximum potential, we must obviously use our whole brain. Because words generally are processed by the left brain, and drawing is an activity that does not use words, drawing is one of the rare activities that exercises the right brain almost exclusively.

Note: The comments in this book on left and right brain organization are generalizations. Different people have their brains organized differently, as is shown by the fact that some people are naturally left-handed, while some others are naturally ambidextrous. Some activities performed by one hemisphere, can sometimes be performed by the other hemisphere also, or both. Science is still learning about brain organization and abilities.

DRAWING HELPS YOU BE CREATIVE & SOLVE PROBLEMS

Creativity and imagination come primarily from the right brain. The right brain is also much better than the left brain at seeing "the whole picture".

Therefore, to improve the quality of life, everyone should actively seek activities that stimulate the right brain, and drawing is a most important part of this.

On the other hand, most left-brain teaching makes us compartmentalize things and see only part of the picture, without any relationships between the different parts. Also, the left brain is not good at coming up with new ideas, and it is very critical and much more likely to put a person down and stop them from doing anything.

While the left brain likes to belittle right-brain thinking, the left brain can be slower in working things out. The left brain tends to see things in a linear, sequential, logical, step-by-step manner. Everything is separate from everything else. For example, history is separate from geography, even though the two are often highly related to each other.

While the left-brain is more time-oriented than the right brain, the left brain can be a lot slower in the way it thinks. It goes "A leads to B which leads to C so the answer must be ... D". On the other hand, the right brain sees the whole, 3-dimensional aspect of everything, and especially sees how everything is related to everything else. The right brain, using intuition, can immediately go "A leads to D!", without having to view the intermediate steps. Developing your right brain is valuable for increasing your awareness of life, and seeing when problems are present, and then solving them with creative new solutions. So far as I know, the theory that learning to draw helps people to do creative problem solving was first put forward by Betty Edwards, author of *Drawing on the Right Side of the Brain*. She does an excellent job of proving this point, and in fact makes a living out of teaching highly successful, professional people to draw, in order for them to solve problems at work.

DRAWING HELPS US TO SEE CLEARLY

While we think we see everything around us clearly, this is not necessarily true. Light comes into the eyes, and stimulates nerves, which sends signals to the brain, which turn the signals into a 'picture'. An example of how we do not always see the truth of what is out there is our blind spot. A part of each eye does not have any light-detecting cells, because the optic nerve is there instead, so the brain later on edits the picture and "fills in the blank" according to what it figures should be there. If a person is driving and a car behind them happens to be in the blind spot, when they look in the rear view mirror, the brain may edit the car out.

Incoming data is also edited by the left brain according to a person's past experiences. Sometimes learning to draw and increasing the power of the right brain, enables one to see the truth of what is around us, more clearly, because the right brain perceives and accepts things the way they are, while the left brain changes the information to fit its programs.

For example, the left brain thinks in terms of simple symbols. It 'knows' that a drawing of a house looks like this:

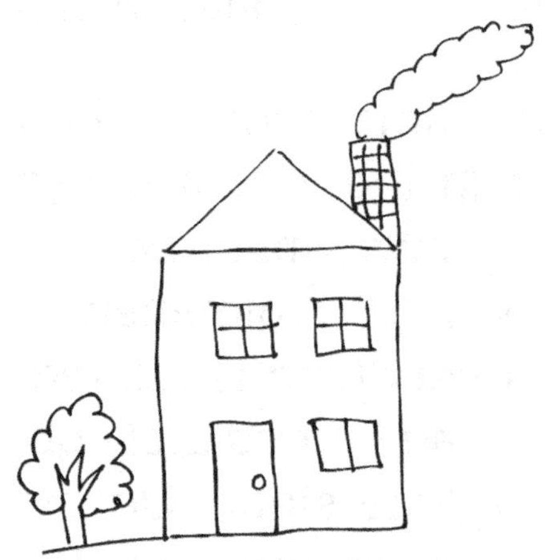

But the right brain simply looks at all the lines and how they relate to each other, and ends up with a drawing like this:

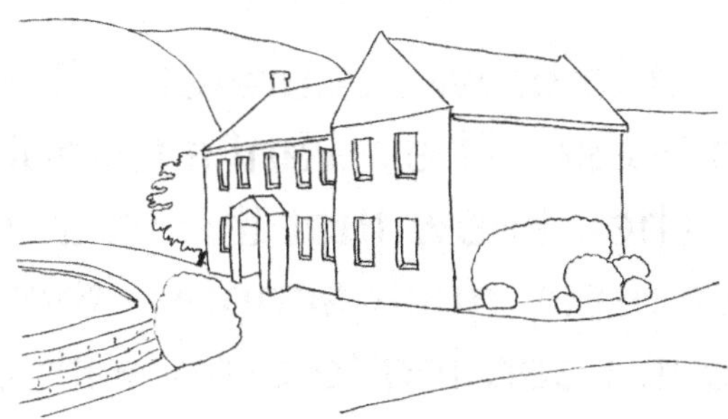

What differences do you notice between these two pictures? A major difference is that the left brain picture is 2-dimensional, but the right brain picture is 3-dimensional. When you look at something that you want to draw, you have to see it in a special way. Basically, you have to pretend that you just photographed it so that it is on a flat, 2-dimensional surface, and then trace over the lines. Those lines will not go where your left brain imagines they go. The left brain tends to see things in terms of symbols, rather than the truth. Again, the left brain 'knows' that a drawing of a horse is a bunch of simple symbols:

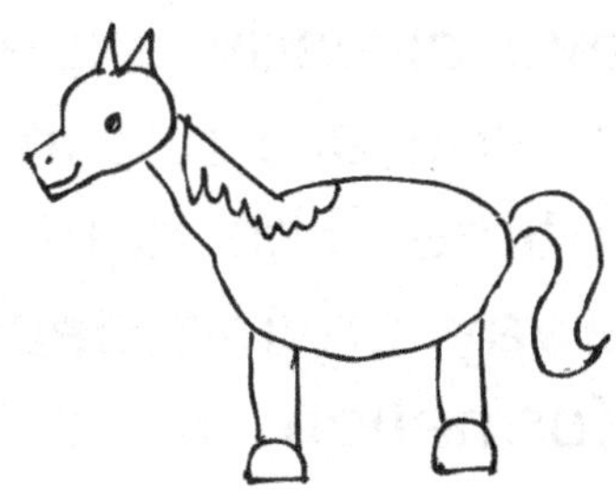

But the right brain looks at every single line and recognizes the truth:

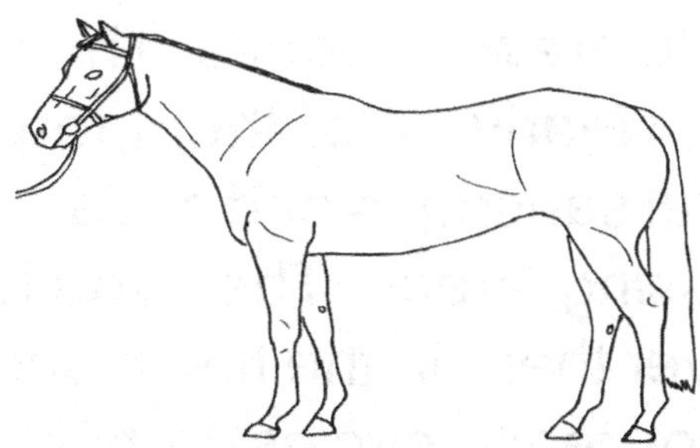

Later one could apply shading to make this drawing even more solid and realistic, and to give more depth, but you have to learn how to do accurate lines before you can do shading.

Nearly all children want to draw accurately. They don't want to draw a simplified symbol of a horse. They want it to look like a real horse. Children are very smart. They know that the truth is important. They also probably know that it's really quite simple – they just want someone to show them how to do it. Learning to draw with grids teaches that skill.

DRAWING HELPS YOU TO BE CALM

If you are feeling a bit stressed, try drawing. If you have children who are a bit hyperactive, teach them to draw. Artists speak of "feeling transported", "at one with their work"… "Awareness of the passage of time fades away and words recede from consciousness. Artists say that they feel alert and aware yet are relaxed and free of anxiety, experiencing a pleasurable, almost mystical activation of the mind." (Ref: *Drawing on the Right Side of the Brain*). Others have described this feeling as a feeling of bliss.

All of this comes from activating the right brain, without intrusion from the left brain. You may have already experienced this feeling when driving on a freeway, when you are not in a hurry to get anywhere, and so are not focused on time. The right brain has little awareness of time. Like drawing, freeway driving deals with visual images, relationships and spatial information, so it activates the right brain.

MOST 'LEARN TO DRAW' BOOKS ARE USELESS

I remember when I was a child and wanted to learn to draw, and got a bunch of those "Learn to draw…" books. They were all worse than useless. I threw them out. Nearly all of them make you see a horse as a bunch of circles and oval sausages and squares somehow tied together. Then you fill in the 'missing' areas. Then you have to erase the parts of the circle that were never there in the first place. Then somehow redraw the areas that were not really circles to begin with. That's ridiculous!

What they are trying to do is get you to see things that just aren't there. The outline of a horse is the outline of a horse. There is no part of a horse that is a perfect circle. And if there was, what happens when the animal turns a bit? Animals and people are not geometric. They are composed of wondrous, artistic curves. A horse has nothing whatsoever to do with ovals or sausages! It was not until I found some learn-to-draw-with-grid books that I finally learned to draw. Here are some examples of how *not* to draw:

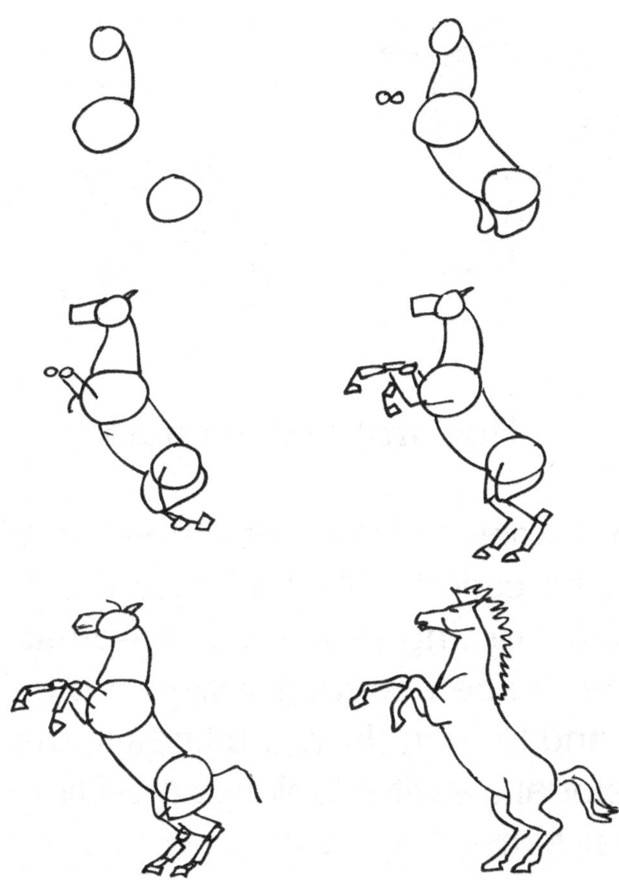

How ***not*** to draw a horse

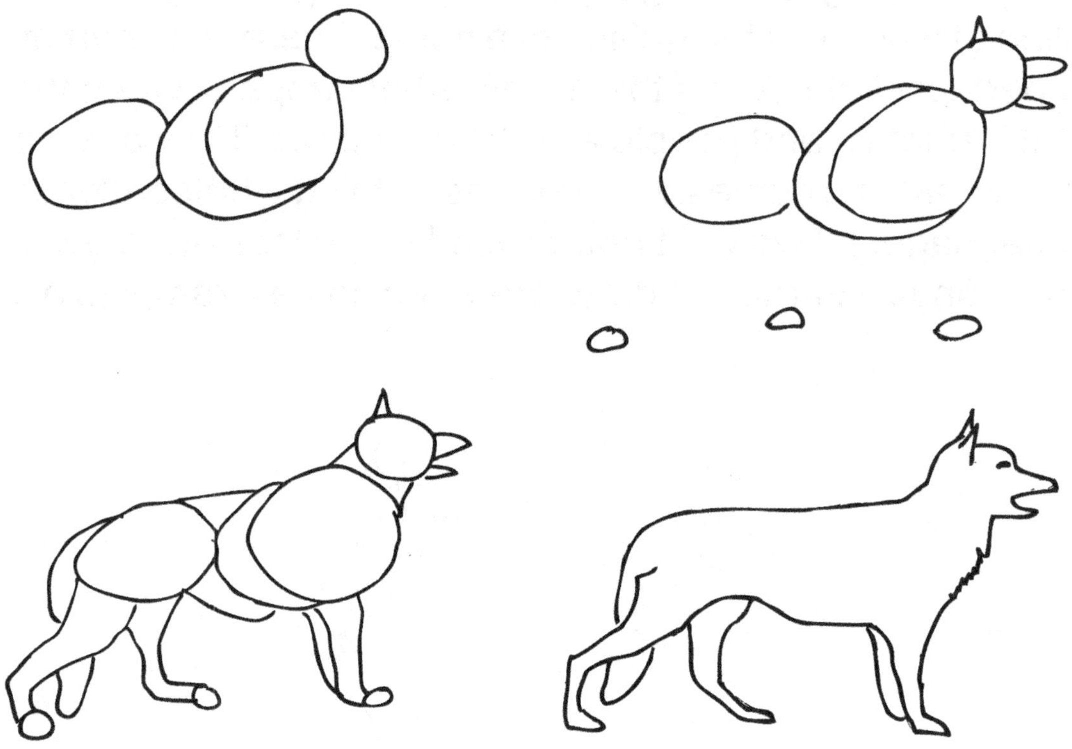

How ***not*** to draw a dog:

The "Learn to Draw" books that don't use these stupid circles and blocks, could just as easily be called "What a horse looks like" or "What a dog looks like". Teaching drawing requires step-by-step lessons. The first step is to learn how to see accurately where the lines are in comparison to each other, and to then draw the lines in the correct position that makes a 2-Dimensional drawing look like a 3-Dimensional object. Then you can just look at something, and draw it, accurately, the first time.

LEONARDO DA VINCI USED GRIDS

The aim of this book is to teach you how to draw accurate, realistic line drawings. When I look back at my childhood to see how I learned to draw, I am sure the main thing was doing grid drawings, like in this book.

Most interestingly, if you have ever wondered how the early art masters created such realistic paintings, many of which look almost like photographs, one of their secrets was that many of them used grids.

Many of these artists considered the use of the grid a trade secret. Leonardo da Vinci was just one of the many artists of his time who used this method for developing an accurate outline of live subjects.

A frame with string or wire was tied horizontally and vertically in such a way as to create a grid. The device was placed between the artist and the model so that the artist could see the subject through the device, enabling the artist to transfer what he saw onto a grid that was drawn on to his paper. Directly in front of the artist's face there would be a kind of "sight" that he would put his nose up against. This would keep his line-of-sight consistent throughout the session. When he was finished with the outline he would complete his painting by using the outline as a kind of map.

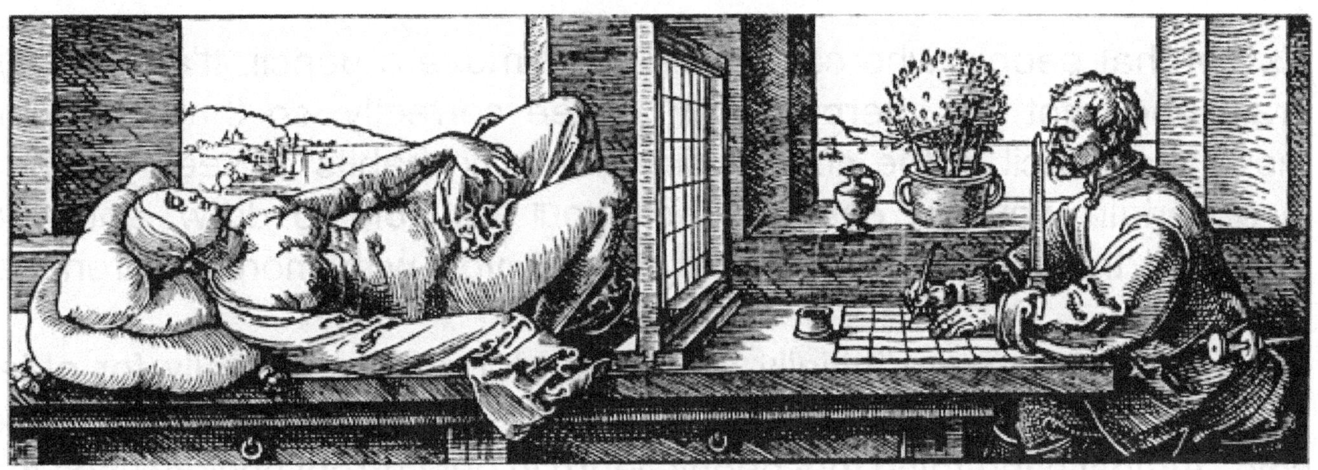

Albrecht Dürer, *Draughtsman Making a Perspective Drawing of a Woman.*
Courtesy of The Metropolitan Museum of Art, New York. Gift of Felix M. Warburg, 1918.

A modern version of this device is called The Dürer Grid.

Using grids teaches you:

- How to frame everything so what you want fits inside the borders. Too many people start drawing and then find that part of their picture goes outside the borders.

- How to focus on making each line appear accurately, in the right place.

- How to get the left brain out of the way, so that your drawing is realistic. For example, you want to draw a real face with all its interesting shapes, not the simple round circle that the left brain thinks it is.

YOUR BRAIN HAS TO CHANGE BEFORE YOU DRAW WELL

Every time we learn something new, we go through what is called a "learning curve". This is the time at the beginning of learning something new when everything can seem tough. This is often because your brain does not yet have the pathways through its nervous system that it needs to do the activity. Keep going. Your brain will start to make those pathways. When the paths become well trodden, the thing you have been learning will suddenly become easy, and as long as you exercise those pathways once in a while, it will stay easy for the rest of your life.

It's not that people who can't draw can't move a pencil. It's that their brain does not yet interpret how to see correctly, so that they can move the pencil in the correct direction. Old habits of seeing things in a certain way will change once you are able to draw, and you may find that you see the world around you with more awareness.

Learning to draw can initially feel uncomfortable, especially for older people, because it uses the right brain, and leaves the left brain out in the cold. Almost everything that people learn in our current society uses the left brain only. You have to wake up sleeping nerve pathways in the right brain before it will start to feel easier, but it will happen if you just keep going.

When this happens, you may also get to appreciate the world around you more. The left brain is very critical. It likes to categorize everything, while the right brain tends to appreciate things for what they are, without judgment.

Keep in mind, before you do as well as you would like, especially if you are an adult where the pathways are more established than they are with a child, you may experience a bit of resistance. Just keep going. It is doing the act that makes the pathways, and eventually makes it easy. An example of this is that it is easier for a person who has already learned a language to learn a second language, than it was for them to learn the first language.

With drawing, you are making more pathways in the right brain, which probably hasn't been used as much as it should. If your brain were a garden, the left brain probably looks well tended, but the right brain looks like a wild jungle – because traditional schooling did nothing to cultivate the right brain. In addition, we want to improve the connections between the left and right brain, because that is what leads to genius.

Each time you do some more drawing, it will be easier, and you will draw better, because in the time between doing drawing, your brain will be busy building and improving new nerve pathways in the right brain. All it takes for you to stimulate those pathways is for you to exercise the right brain by looking at a line and then moving your pencil. That is, doing the drawings in this book.

TIP FOR DRAWING

To start to get your mind thinking in the right way, when you draw a box or cube, it will not look like this –

It will be what is called a "foreshortened square", with sides dropped down to show the height.

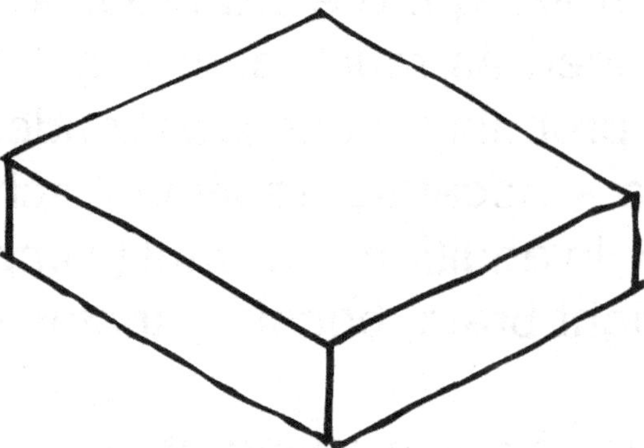

Similarly a round wheel of cheese will not look like this:

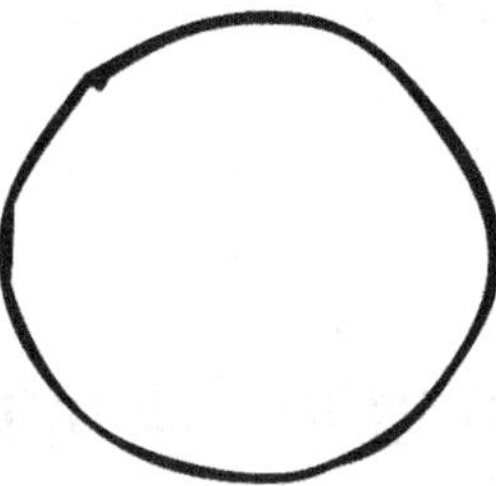

It will be a foreshortened circle, like this, with sides dropped down to show the height:

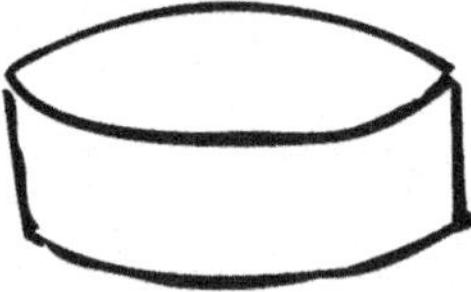

HOW TO HOLD A PENCIL CORRECTLY

It amazes me when I am out in public, at the post office or other places of business, how many people these days do not hold a pen correctly. Apart from the fact that it makes them look uneducated, it makes it much harder to write neatly, let alone to draw. So please make sure that the pencil is always held correctly. It will make it much easier to be accurate, because you will have better control over the pencil. There are various websites that show you this. Here is a good one: www.wikihow.com/Hold-a-Pencil

For young children, you can buy rubber holders that help them to put their fingers in the correct place.

To get started, hold the pencil between thumb and pointer finger only. Then rest the pencil on the middle finger. The thumb and pointer finger should be almost 'kissing' each other. Then move the thumb a tiny bit closer towards the tip than the pointer finger, to take pressure off the pointer finger. Focus on taking pressure off the pointer finger by putting more pressure on the thumb instead avoids heavy writing and 'writer's cramp' – sore muscles.

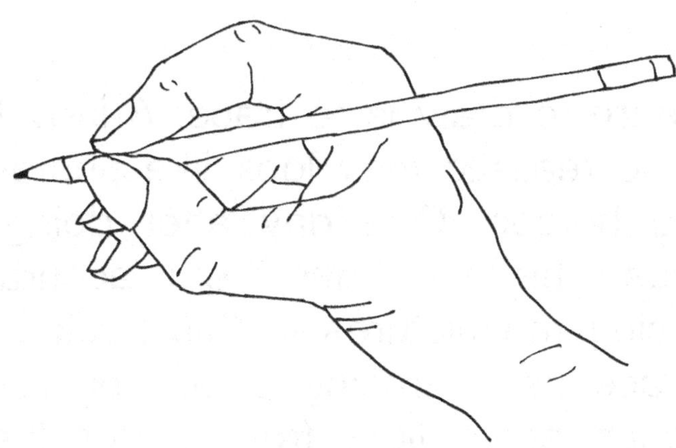

RIGHT HAND OR LEFT HAND?

Different people have their brain organized differently. The best hand to use is the one that you feel most comfortable with. Forcing a child who wants to use his left hand to use his right hand instead, can result in many serious problems, such as stuttering, confusion and difficulty in learning. Left handed people excel in mathematics, music and chess. Famous artists Leonardo da Vinci, Michelangelo and Raphael were all left-handed.

A PERSON WHO IS DRAWING MAY NOT HEAR YOU

When someone is engaged in drawing or painting, their right brain is fully engaged. Words are stored in the left brain, so if you want this person to hear you, do not be surprised if it takes them a while to engage the left brain and 'come out of it' and hear what you have to say. They are not ignoring you or, in the case if a child, being disobedient. It is just that the right brain may be able to hear some kind of noise, but it is not interested in working out what it means, so while the person is drawing, they very likely cannot hear a word that you say, until they have switched back to left-brain mode, which can take a certain amount of time. In our house we say "beep" if someone is deeply engaged in a project, to get their attention, before talking.

DO TRACING

Another way to learn to draw is to trace. A lady I know who paints pictures that are so realistic they look like photos, learned to draw initially by tracing horses. One day after doing this for a while, she suddenly was able to draw them accurately without tracing them. Try tracing the pictures in this book before you use the grids. You can trace using tracing paper, or you can buy a tracing light box, which emits light from under the piece of paper.

MATERIALS NEEDED

1) You will need:

• A pencil. Use an HB or #2 to start with, as it is a good all around pencil.

• An eraser.

• A sharpener.

Pencils with "B" in the name are soft. Pencils with "H" in the name are harder leads. Hard pencils are lighter in tone while soft pencils are darker. The lighter they are, the easier they are to rub out. Later on you may also like to get a graphite stick for shading.

HOW TO DO THIS BOOK

SUGGESTION 1

1) Cover up all of the picture except for one square, with pieces of plain paper. Draw that square in the corresponding position. Notice especially which lines cross the borders of the grid, and where they cross the grid. (Is it in the corner? Half way up? A quarter way up?)

2) Uncover another square next to that square. Keep the rest of the drawing covered up. Draw the second square. You can see enough of the first square you drew, to see where lines are to be joined. Continue doing this until the whole picture is complete.

When you are done, have a look and see what is not right. Then notice what position in the square the lines should be, and correct them.

Surprisingly, if you do this method, rather than draw without covering up any of the picture, the picture may come out better, because the left brain will not know what you are drawing, and so not get in the way of the right brain's ability to just look at lines and work out where they should go.

SUGGESTION 2

Draw the main outline. Notice especially which lines cross the borders of the grid, and where they cross the grid. (Is it in the corner? Half way up? A quarter way up?).

Fill in the other lines.

When you are done, have a look and see what is not right. Then notice what position in the square the lines should be, and correct them.

NOTES:

1) There are blank pages to prevent any bleed through from other pictures, so that they will look wonderful if you cut them out and hang them up.

2) If you have an appointment to keep, I recommend that you set a timer, as time has little meaning when you are drawing. You may be amazed at how fast time flies.

HAVE FUN!

Drawing is fun! Drawing well is even more fun. The sooner you get started, the sooner you will draw well.

Horse

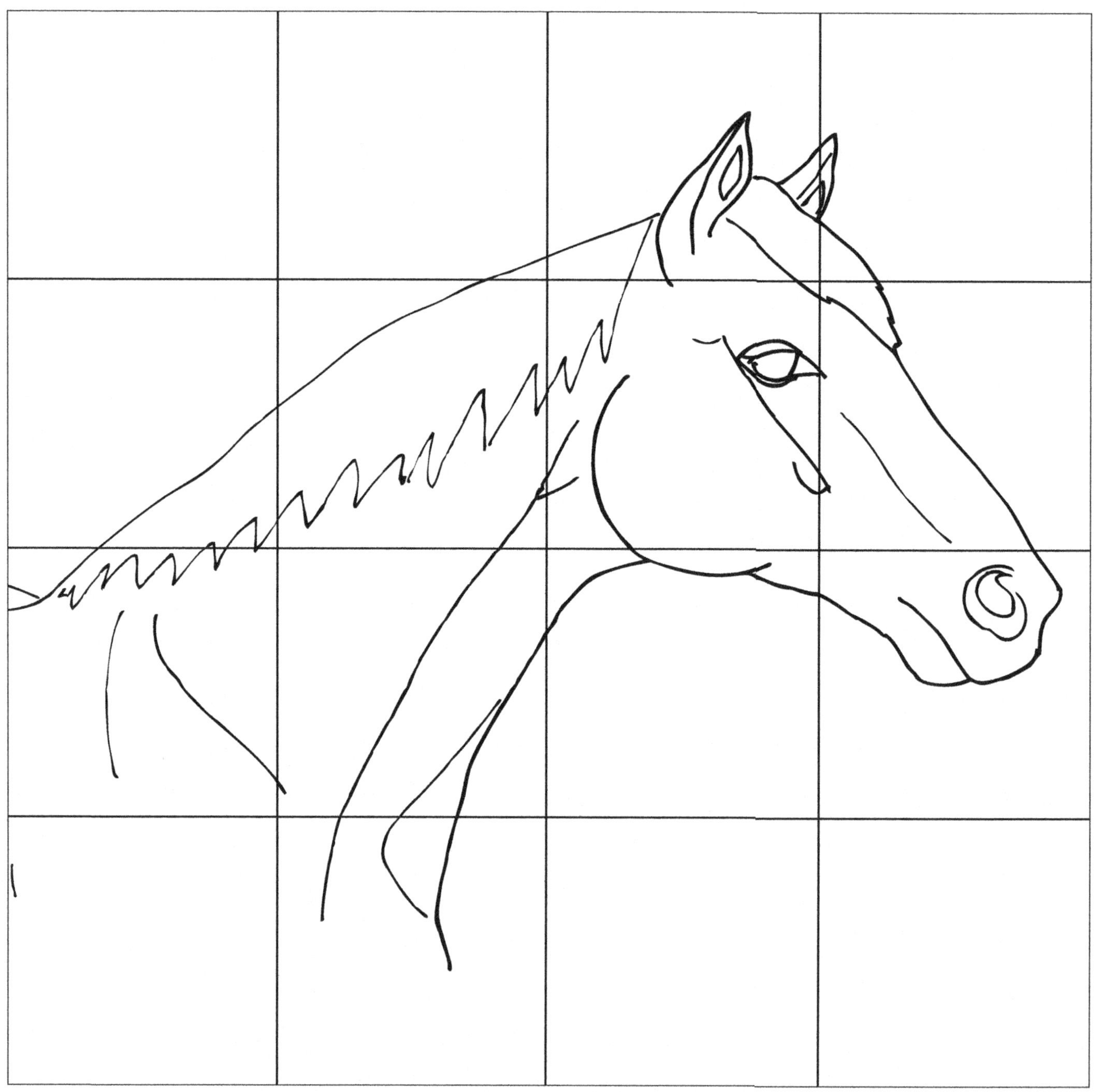

Horse

Polar Bear

Polar Bear

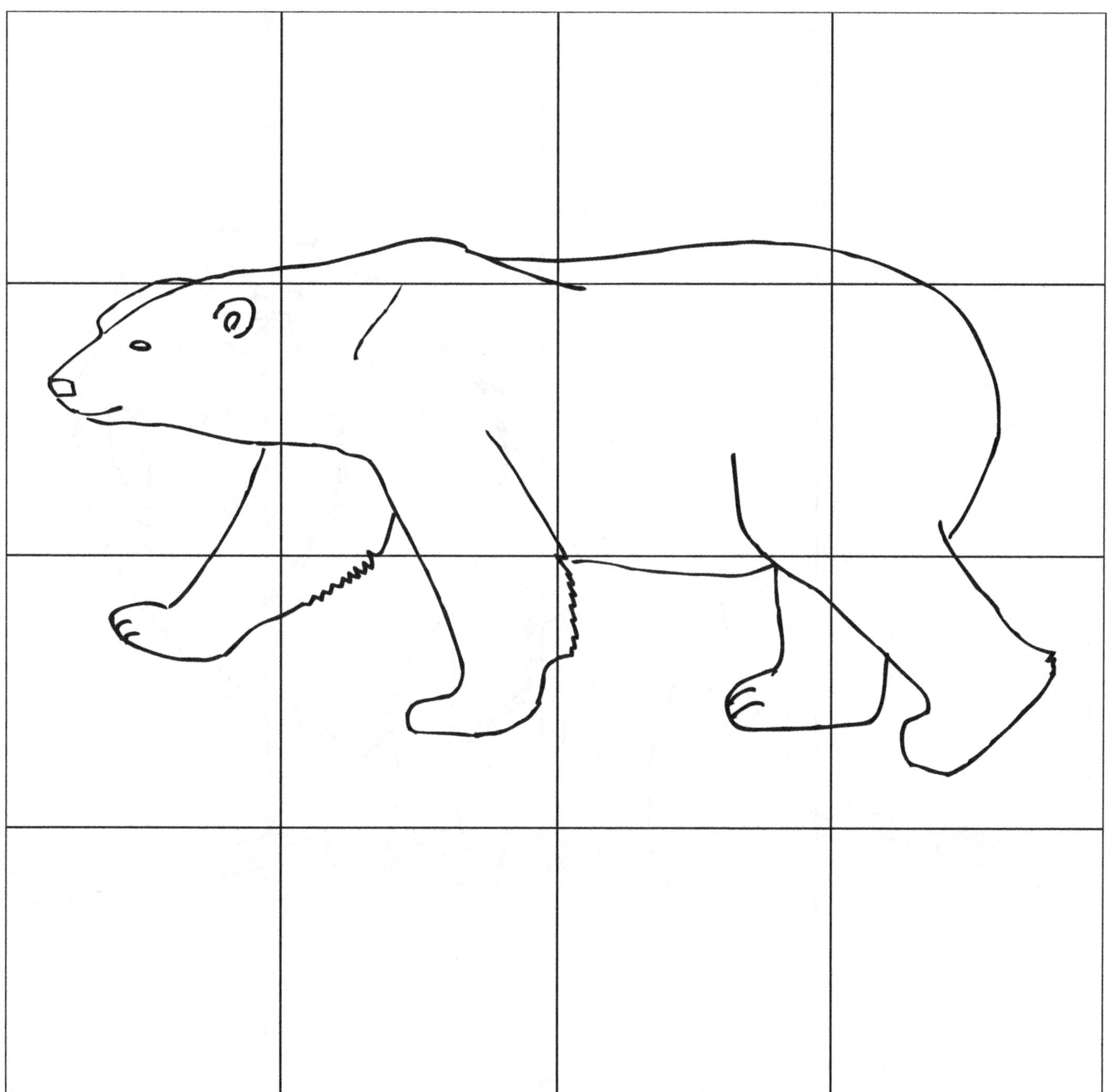

Lion

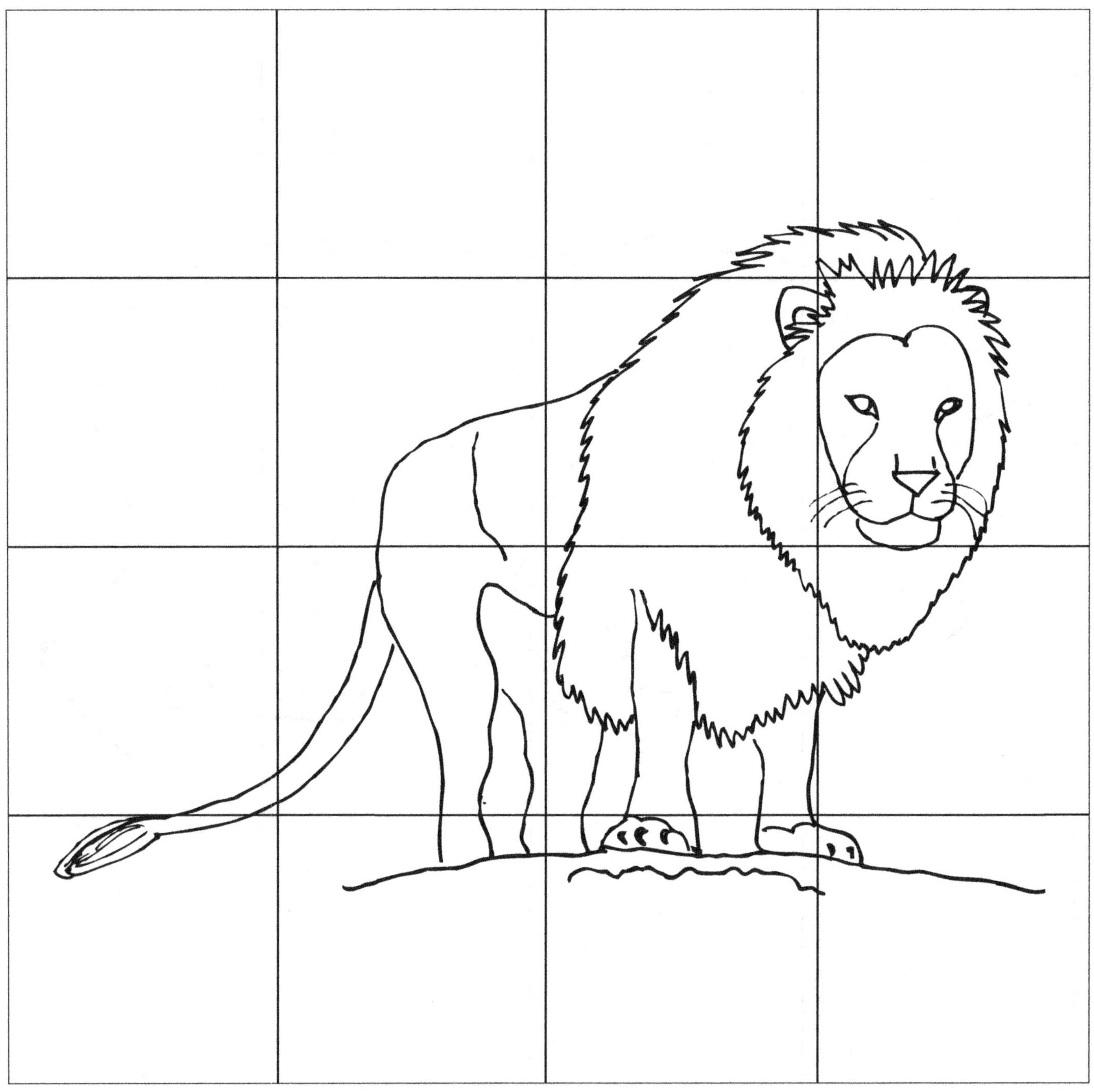

Lion

Bighorn Sheep

Bighorn Sheep

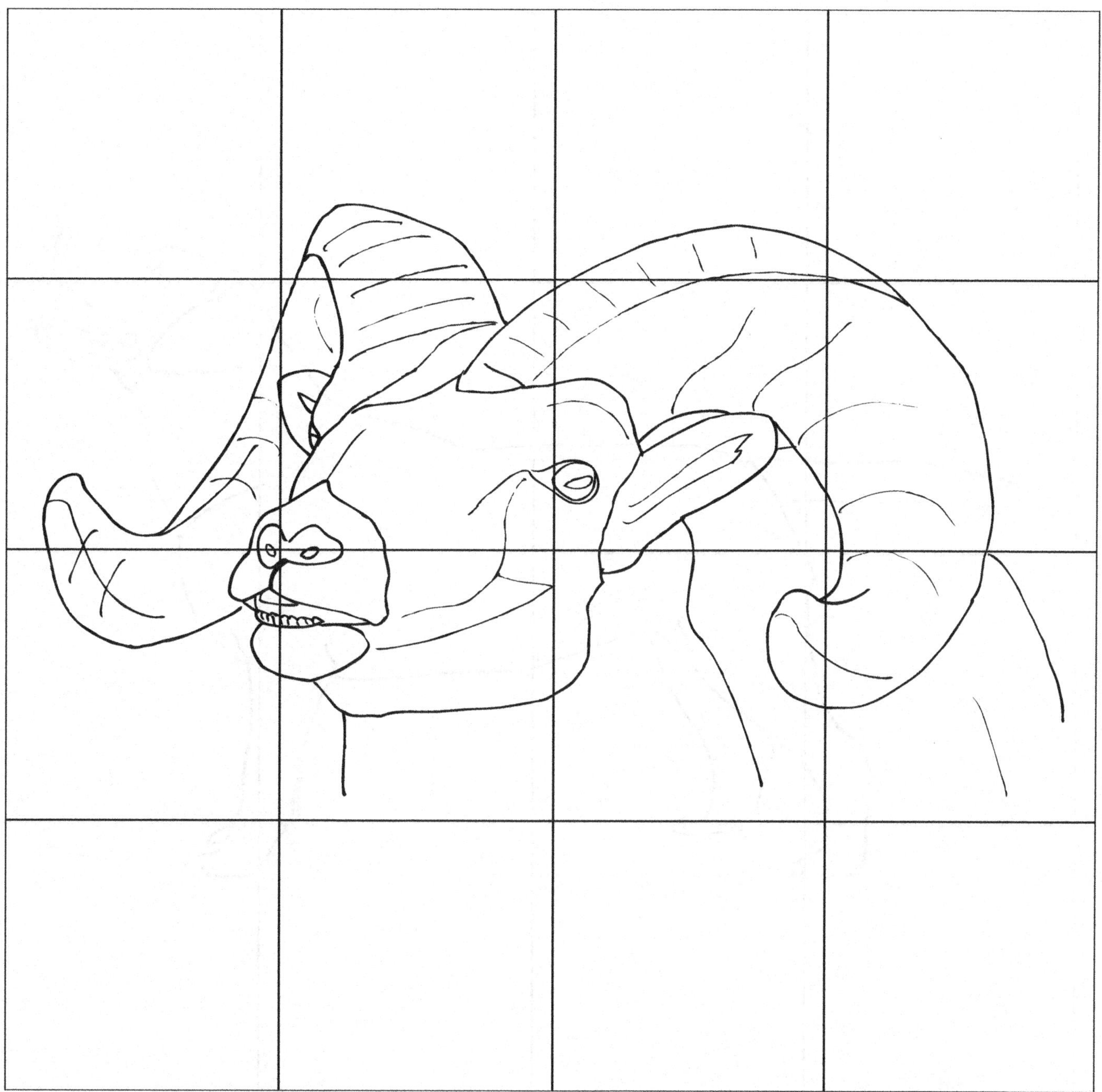

Labrador

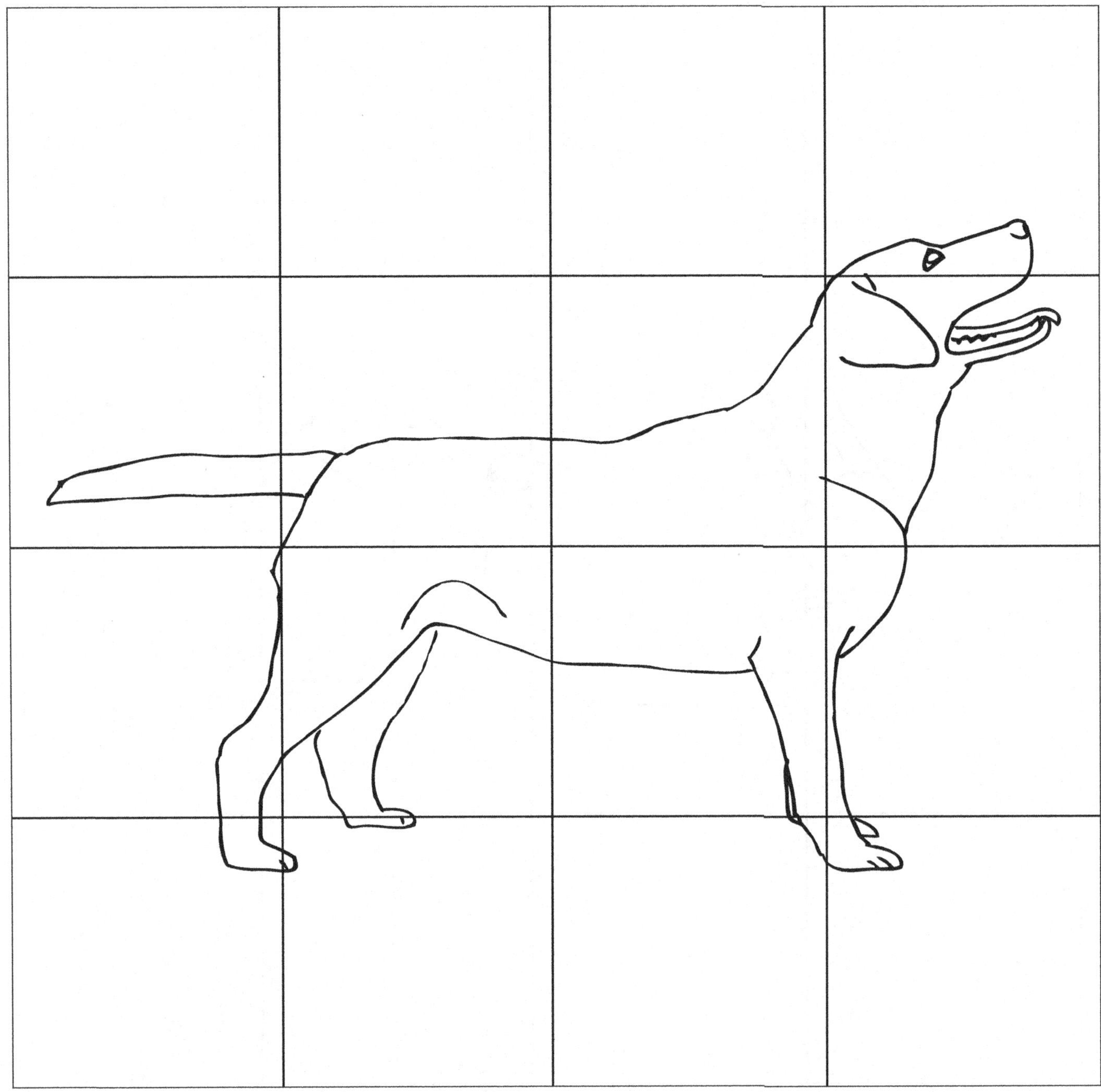

Labrador

Koala

Koala

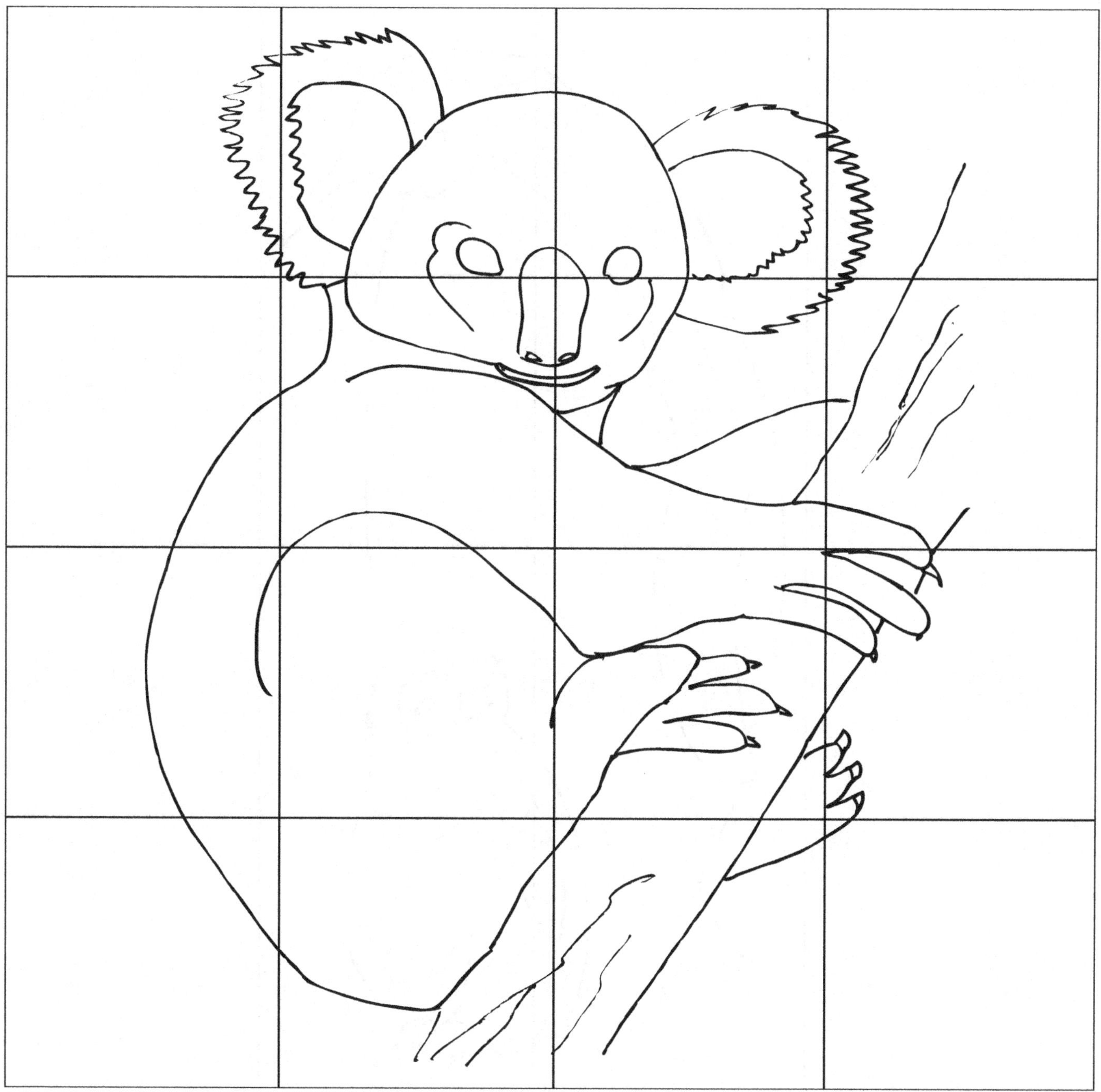

Emperor Penguin

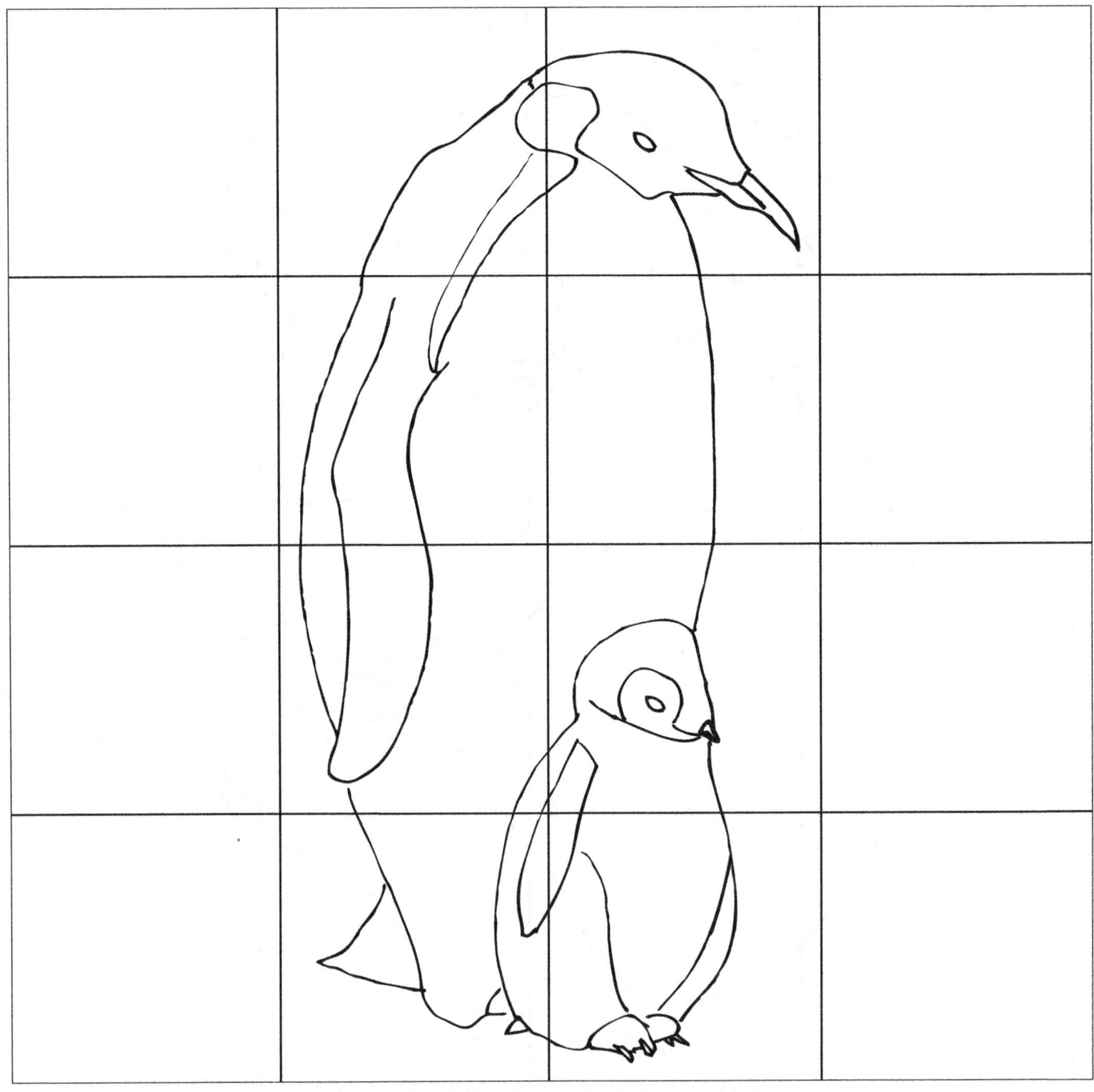

Emperor Penguin

Bactrian Camel

Bactrian Camel

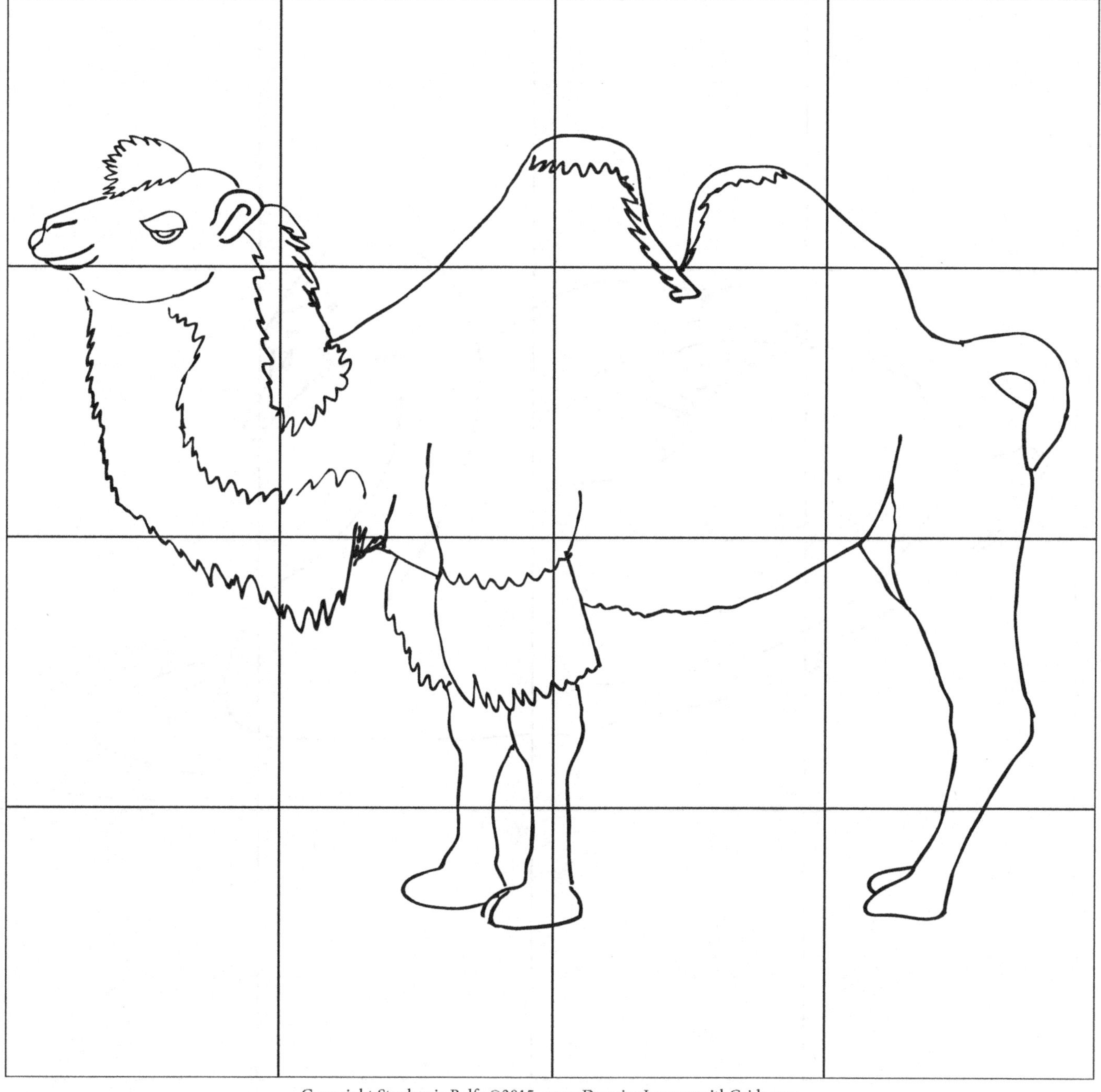

Mute Swan

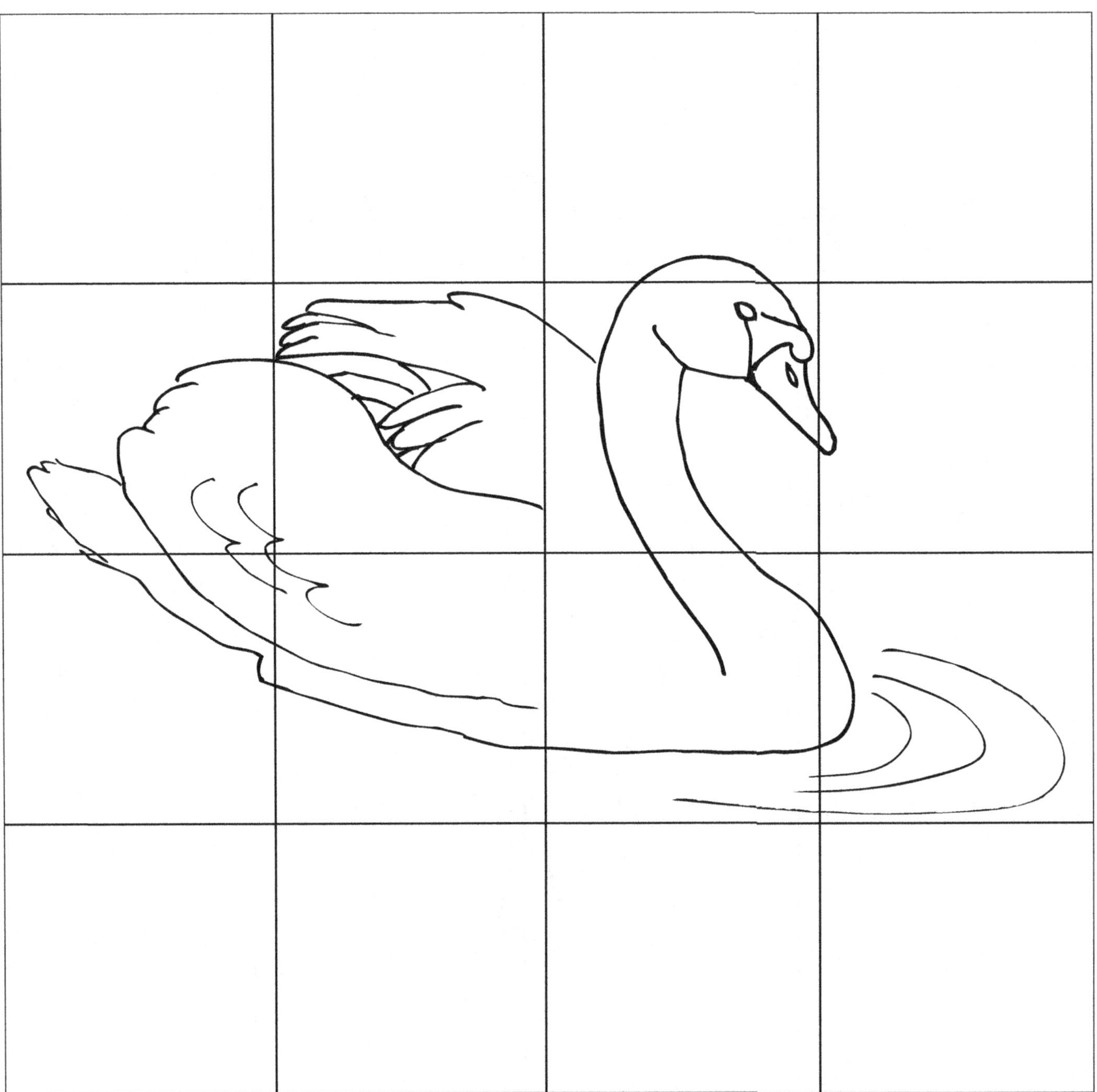

Mute Swan

Swan and Bridge

Swan and Bridge

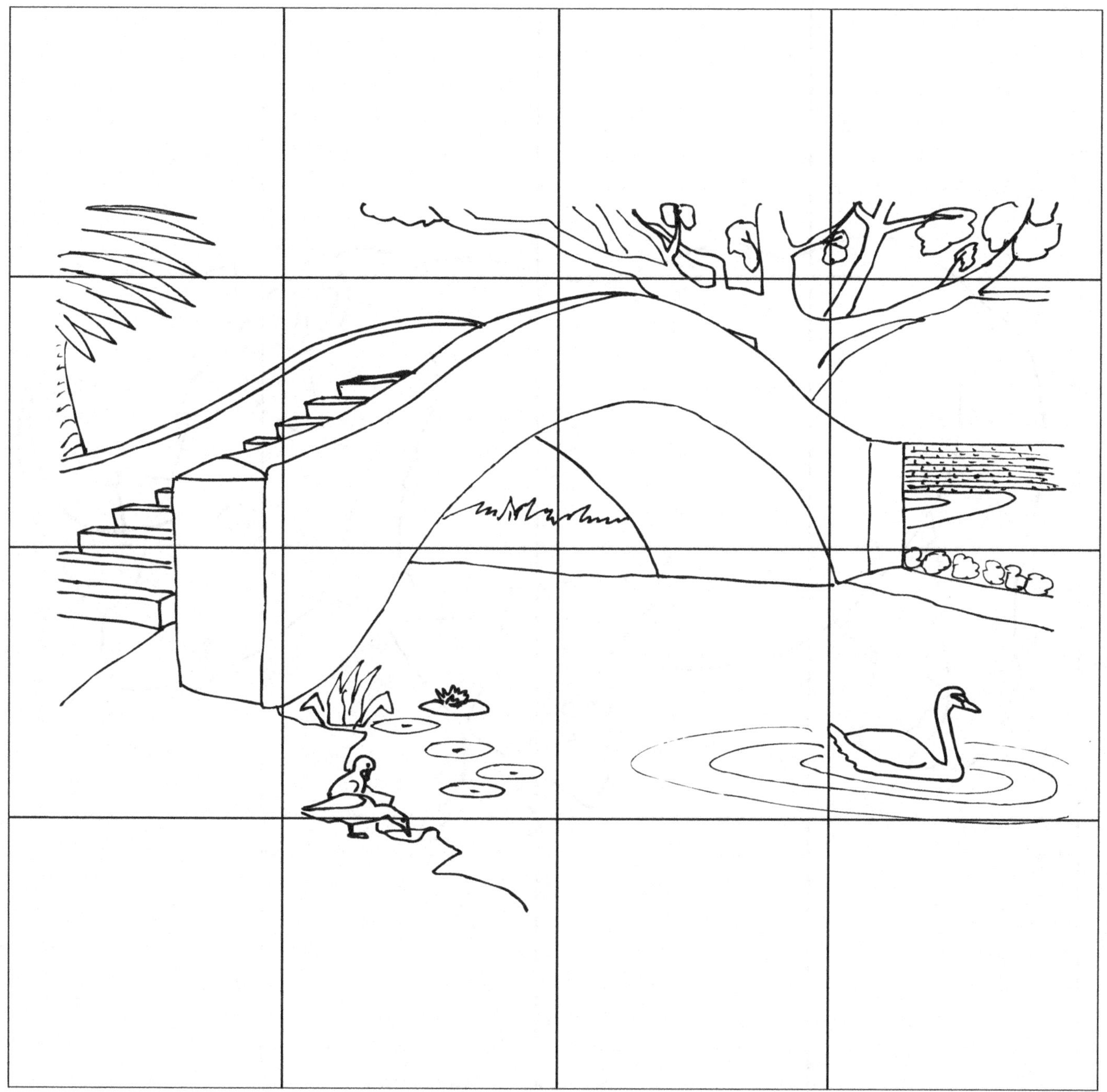

White Rhino

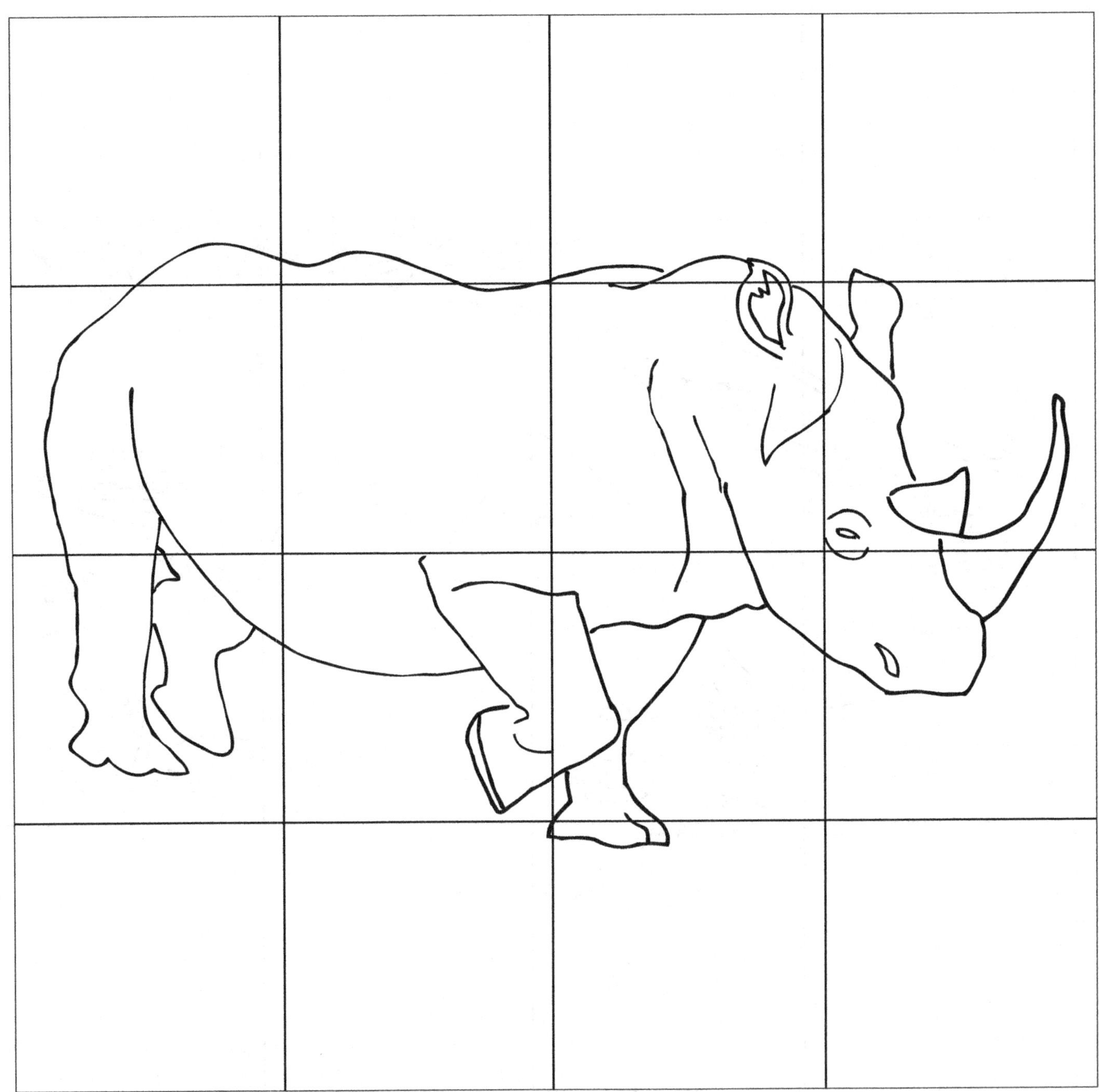

White Rhino

Deer Fawn and Rabbit

Deer Fawn and Rabbit

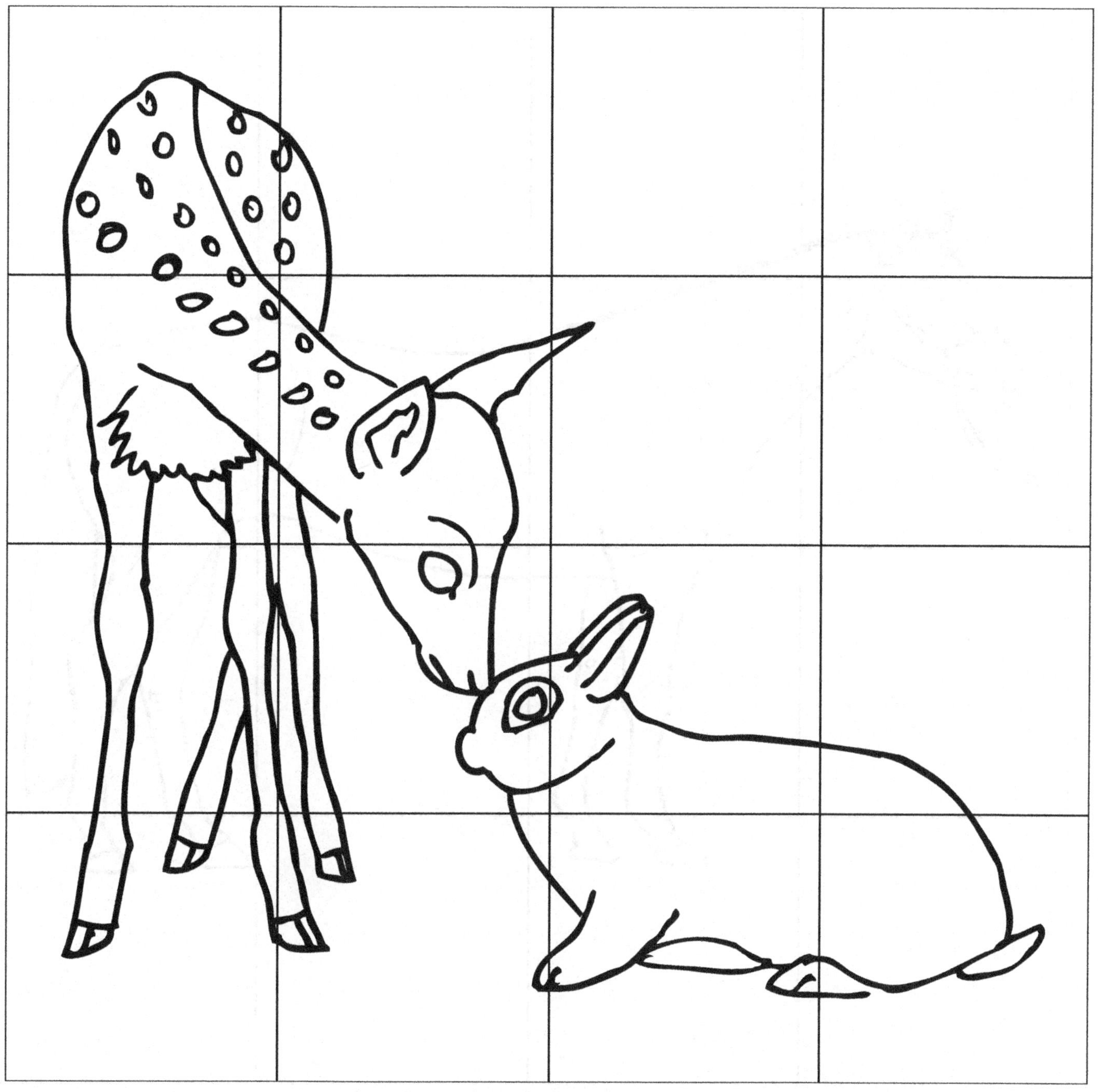

Thoroughbred Horse

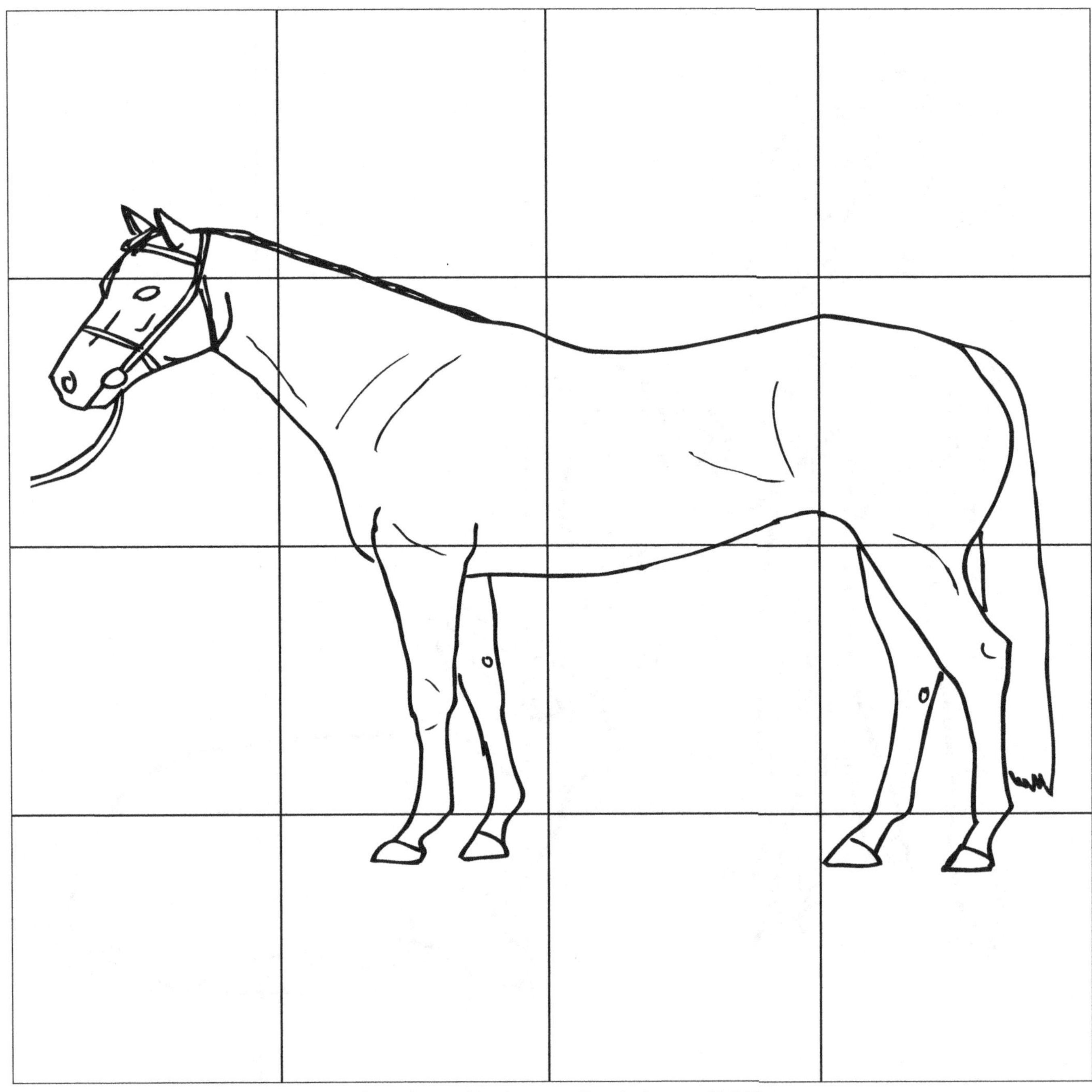

Thoroughbred Horse

Sulfur Crested Cockatoo

Sulfur Crested Cockatoo

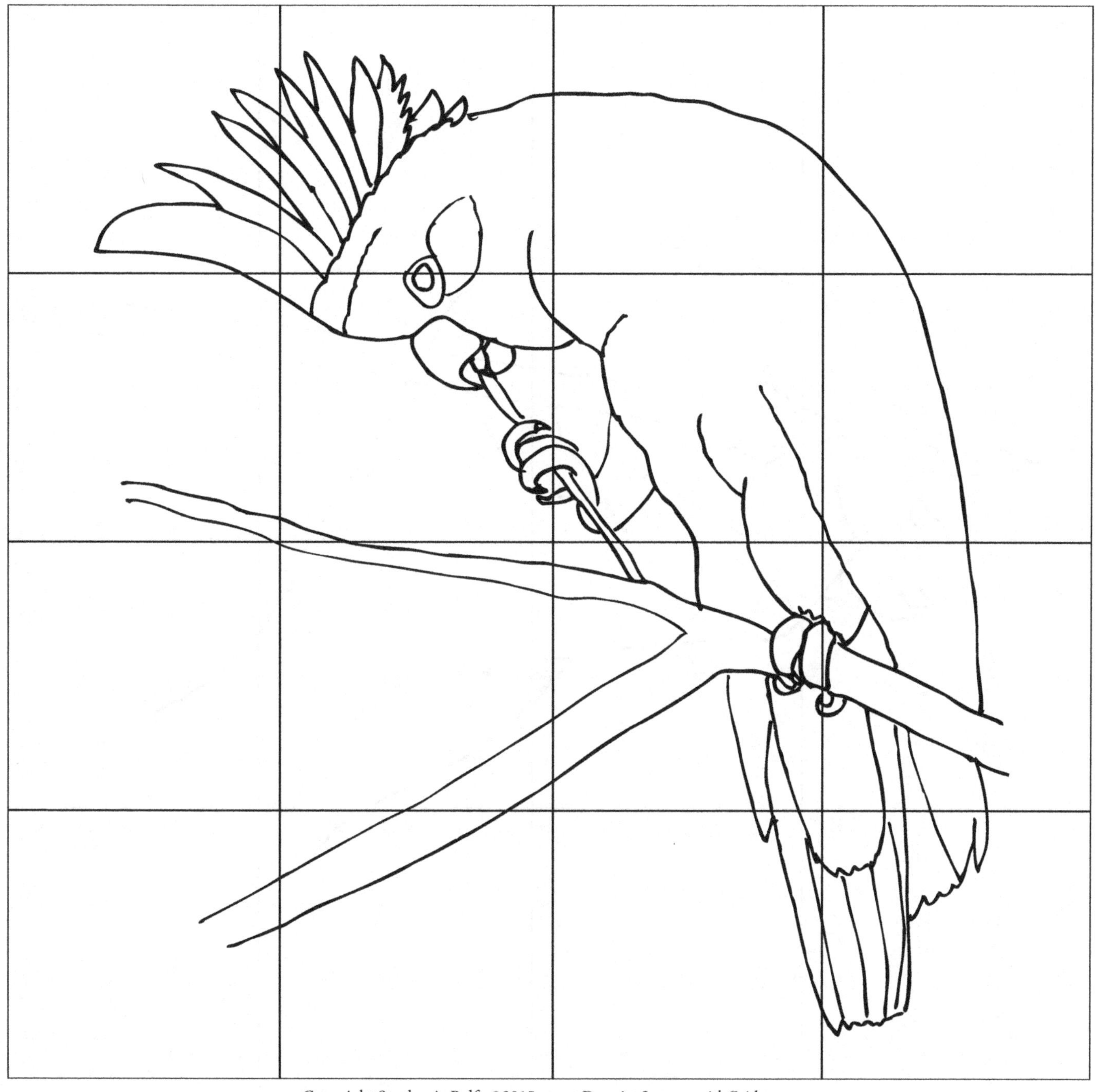

Correct way to hold a pencil

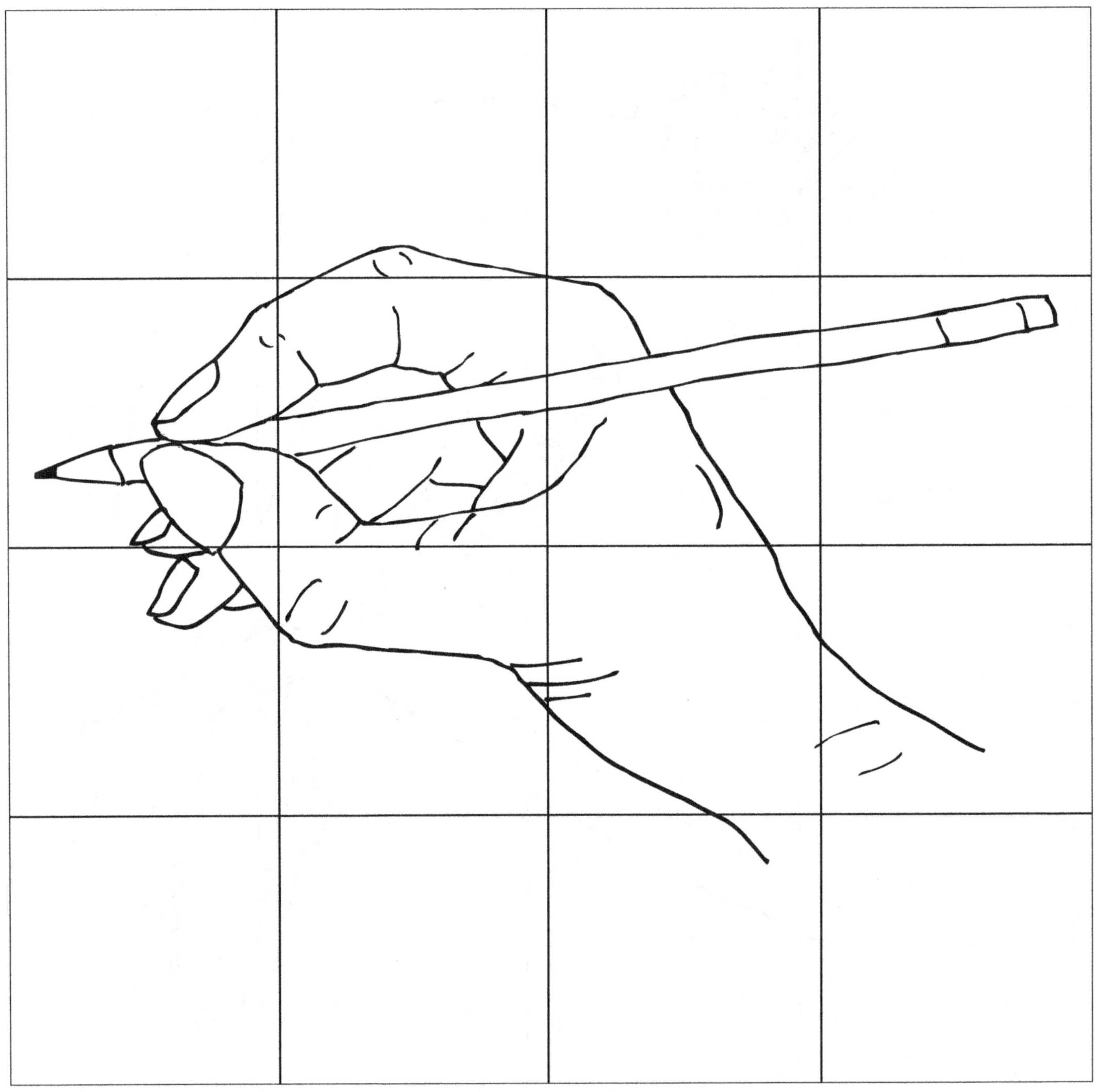

Correct way to hold a pencil

Squirrel

Squirrel

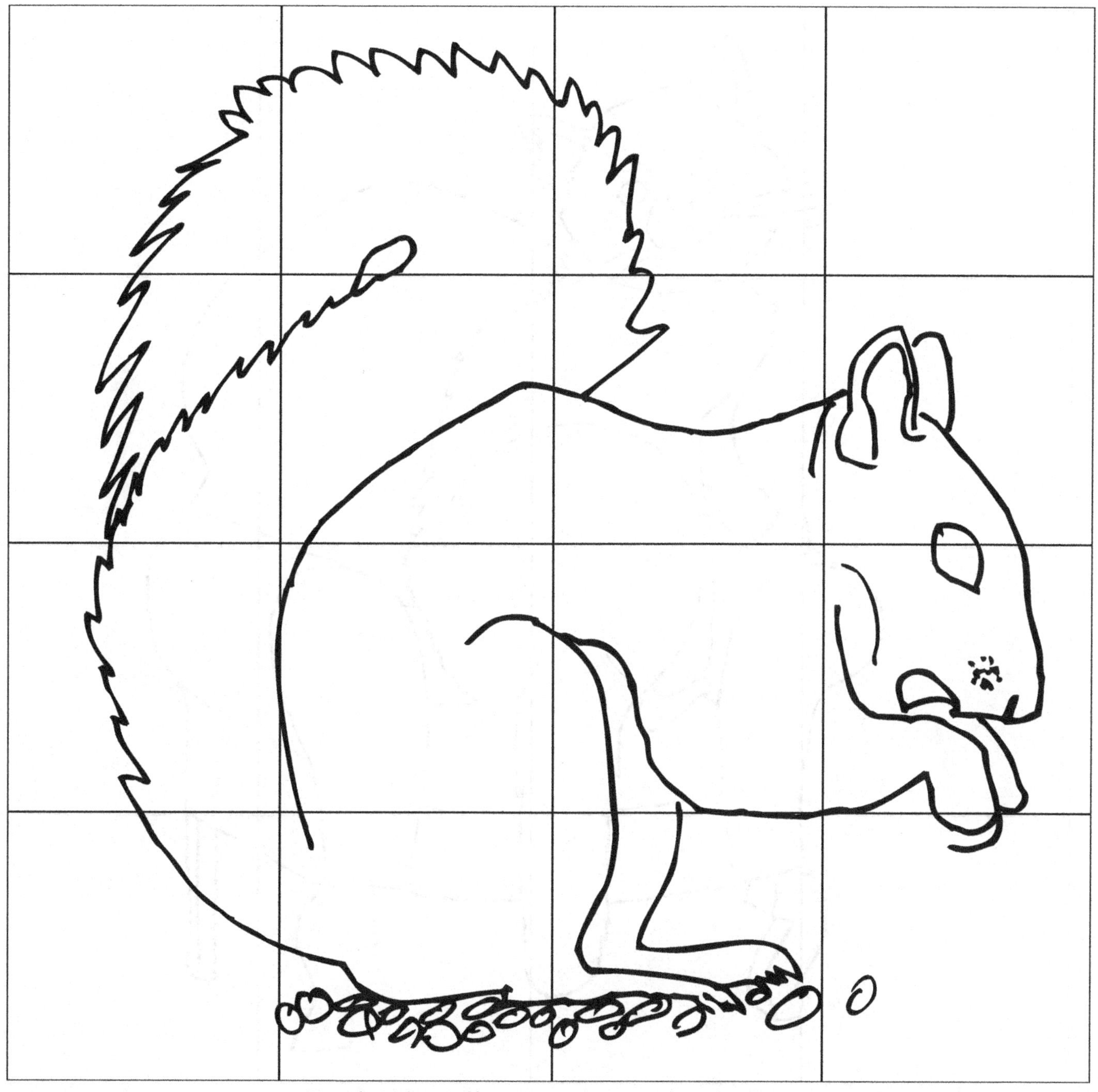

Kitten

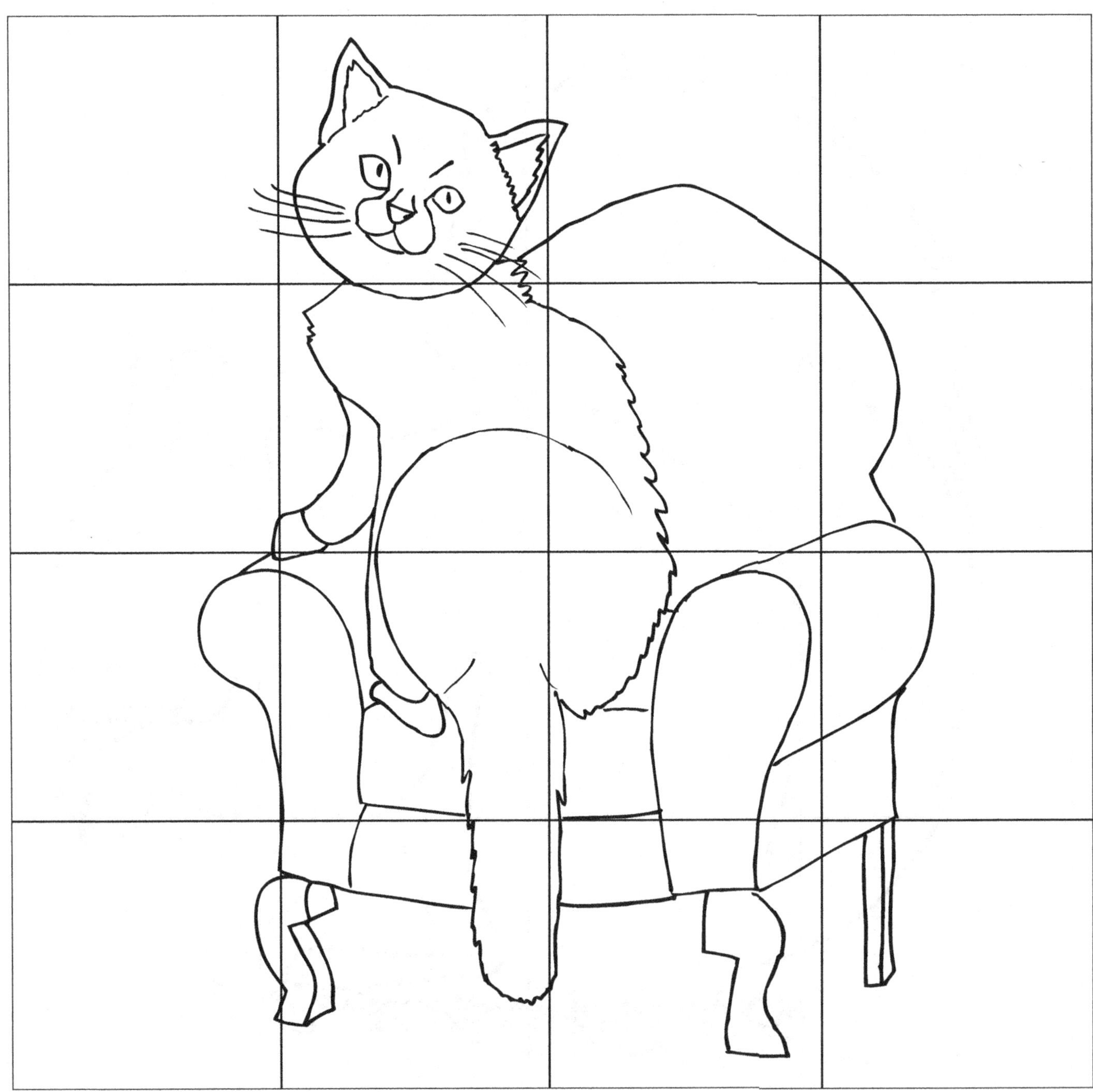

Kitten

Hourglass Dolphin

Hourglass Dolphin

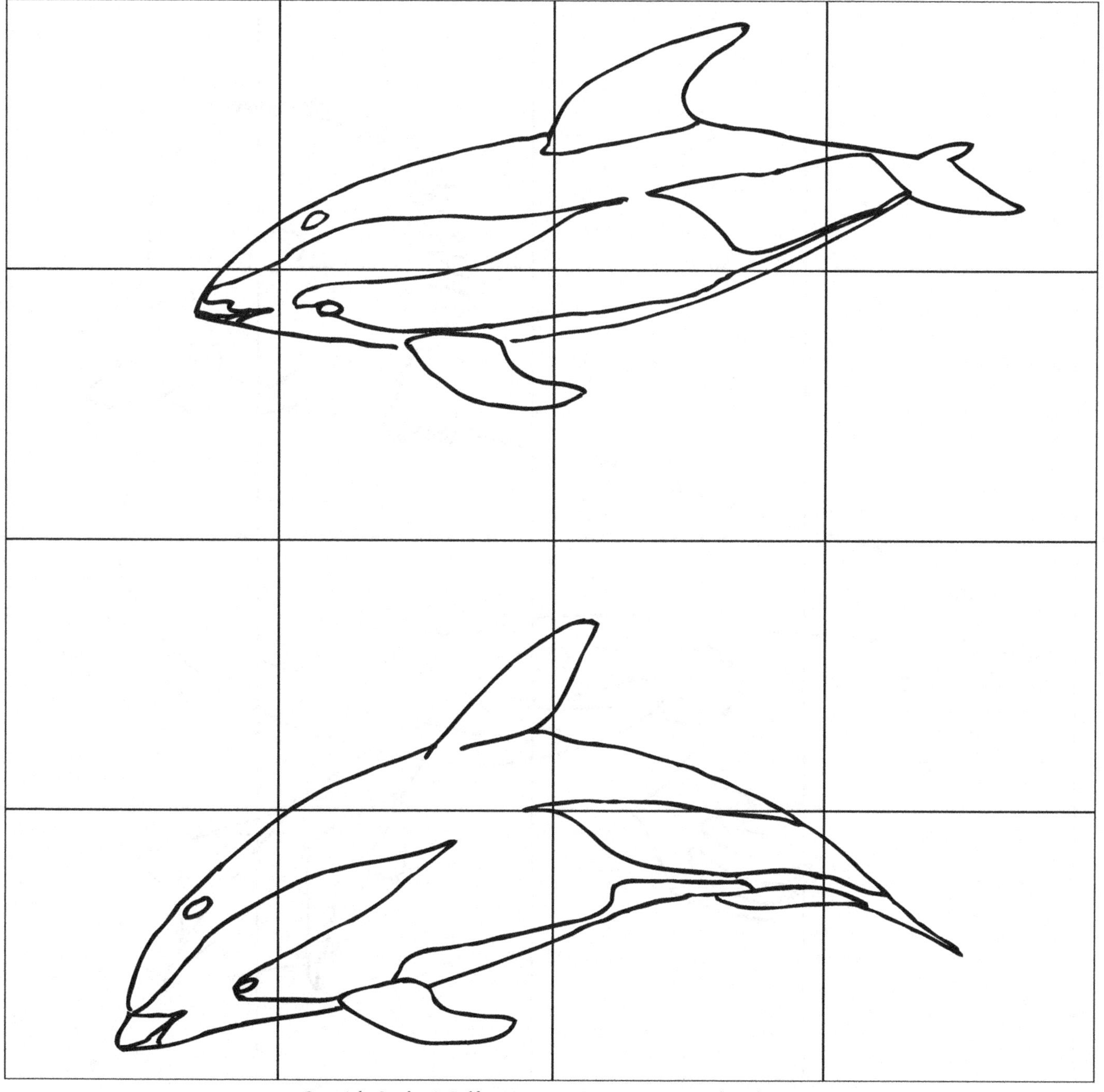

Duckling

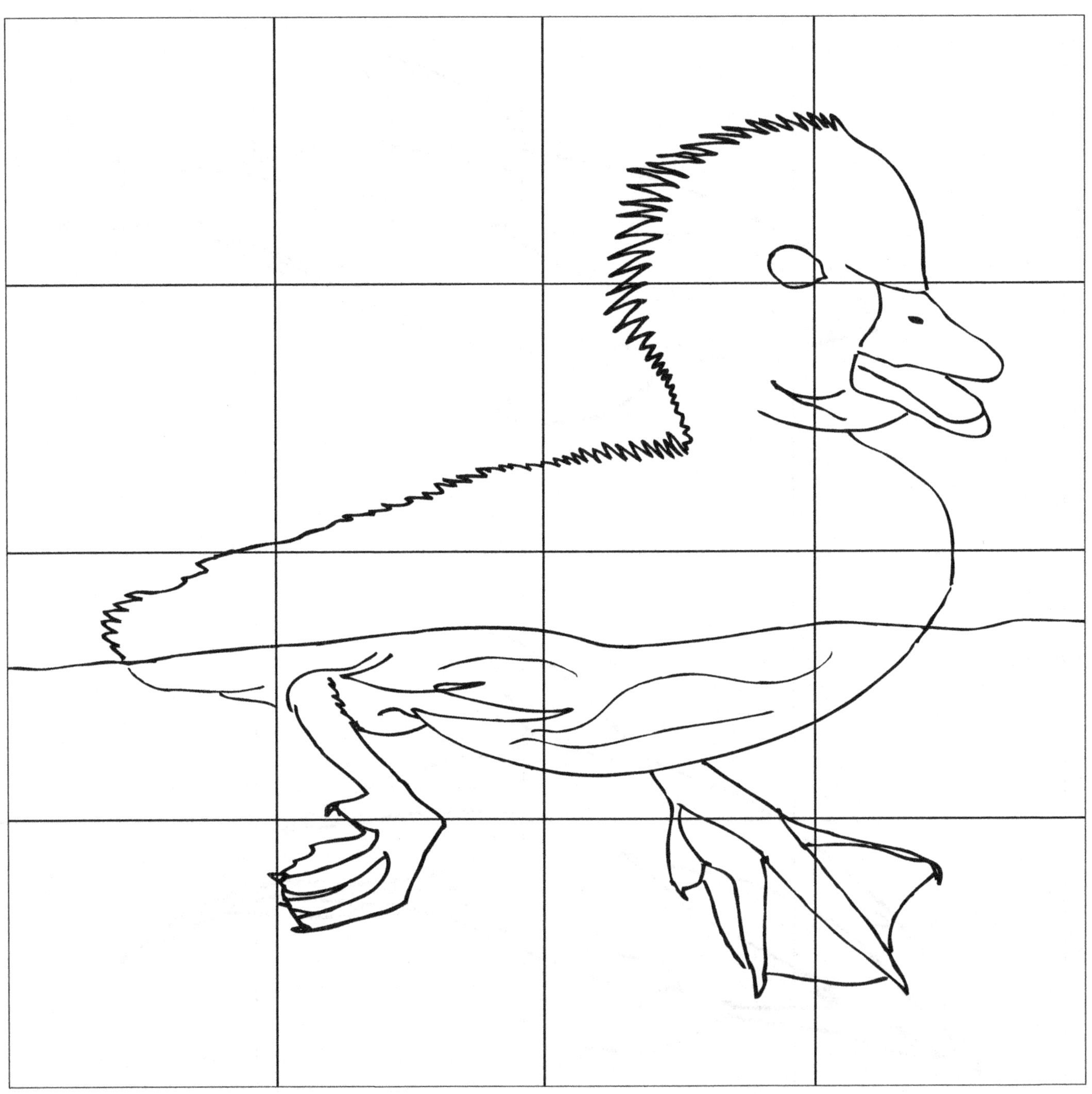

Duckling

Eagle

Eagle

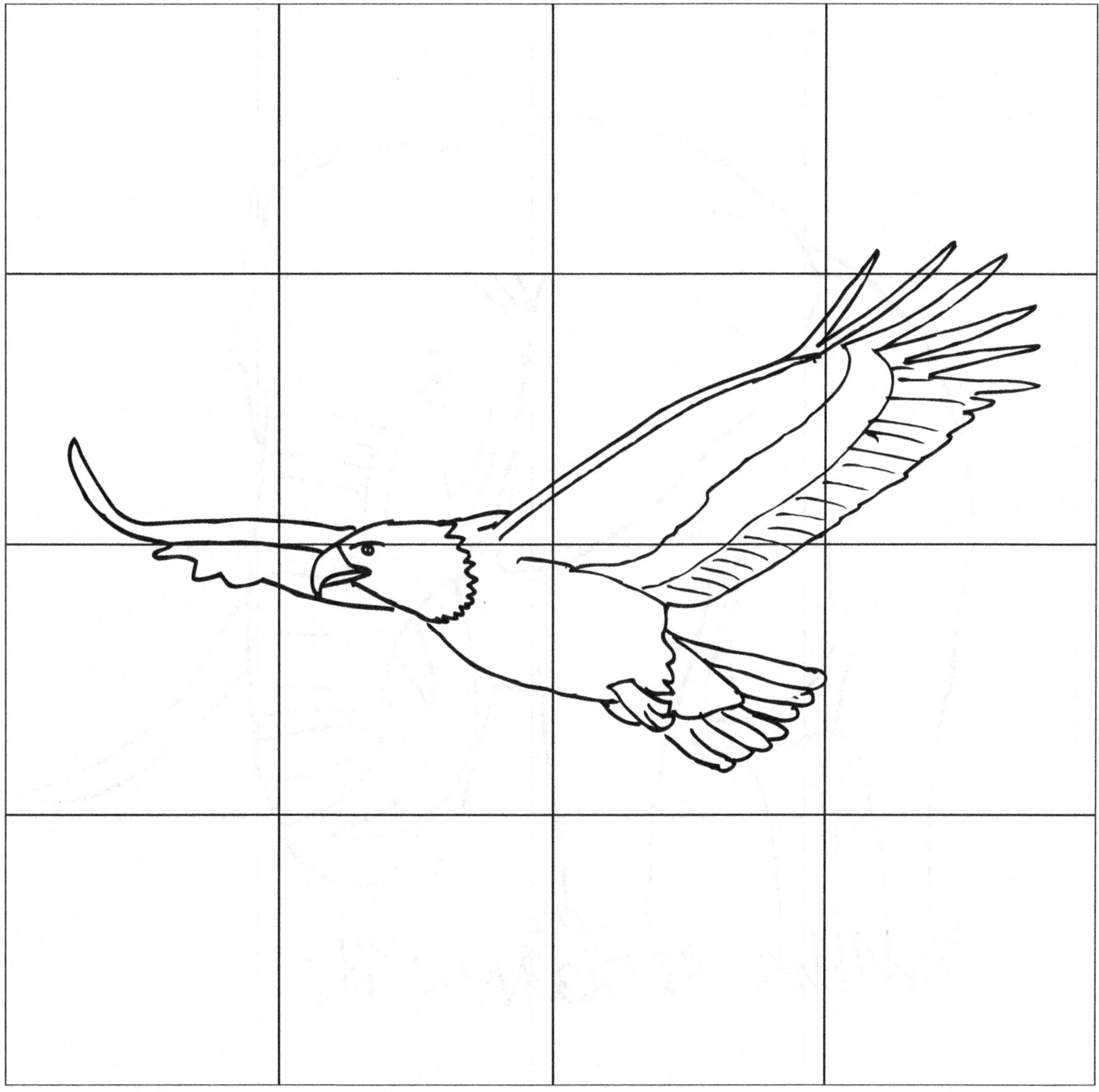

Elephant

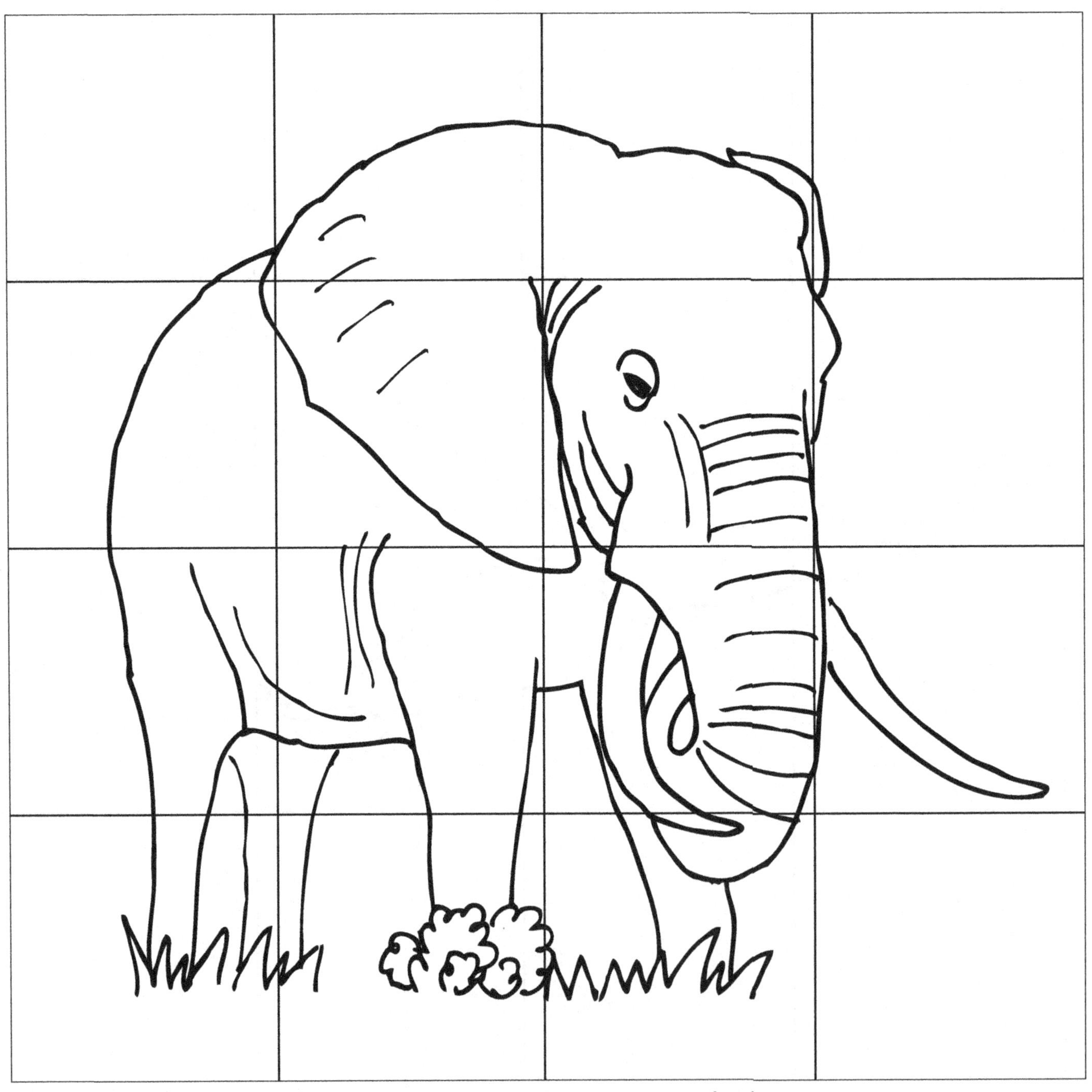

Elephant

Caribbean Reef Shark

Caribbean Reef Shark

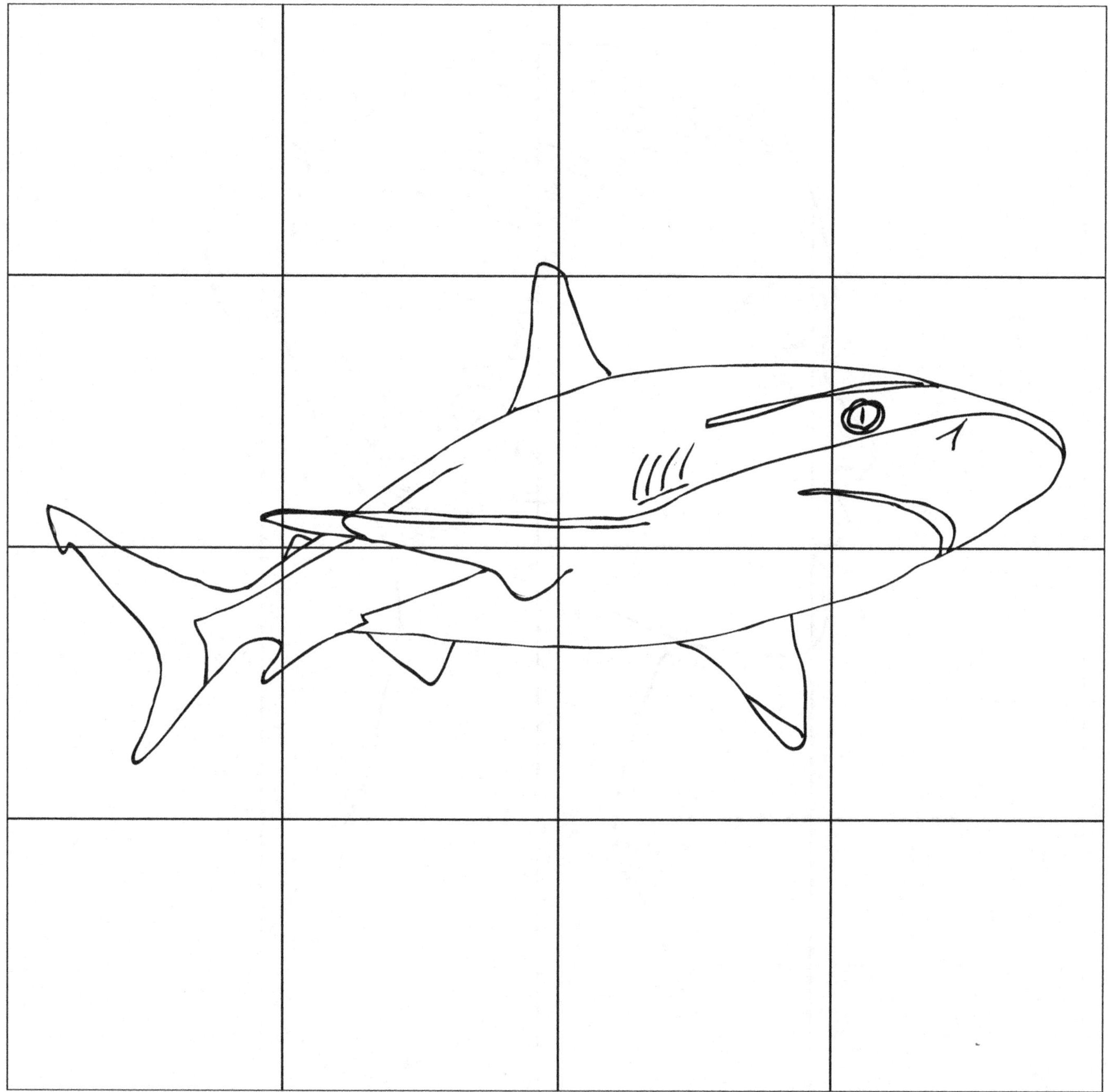

Elegant Lady

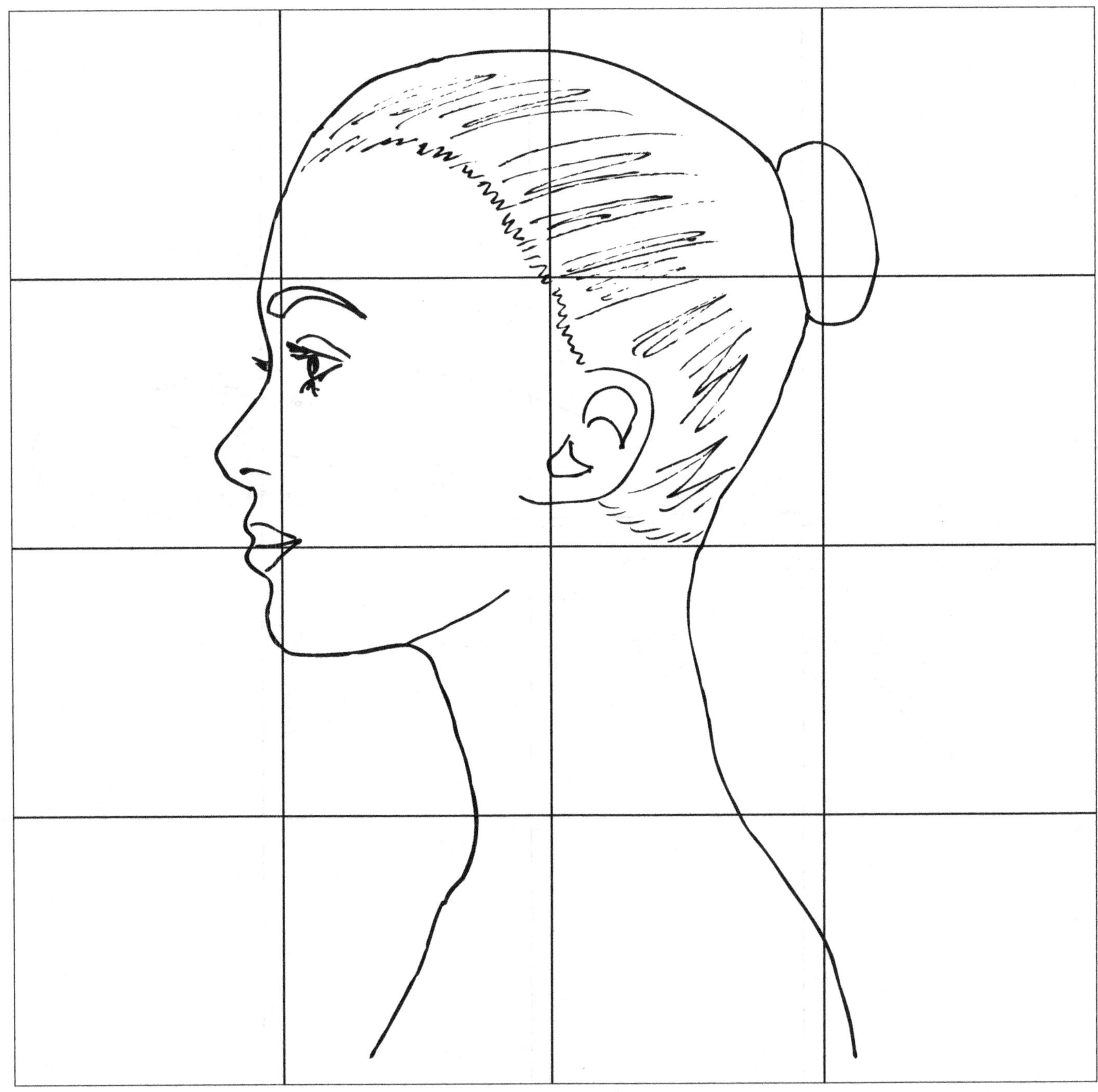

Elegant Lady

Clownfish

Clownfish

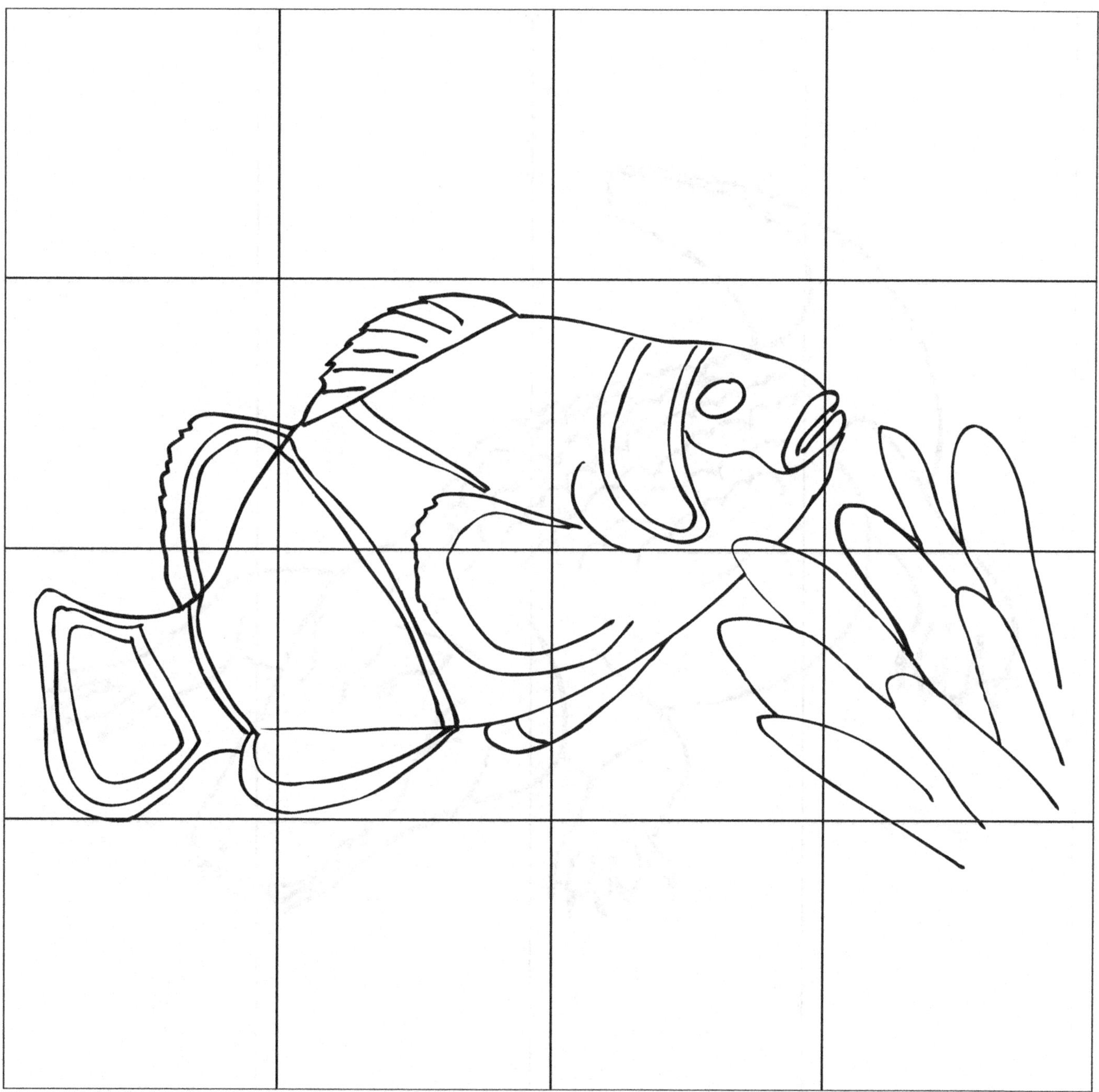

Alligator

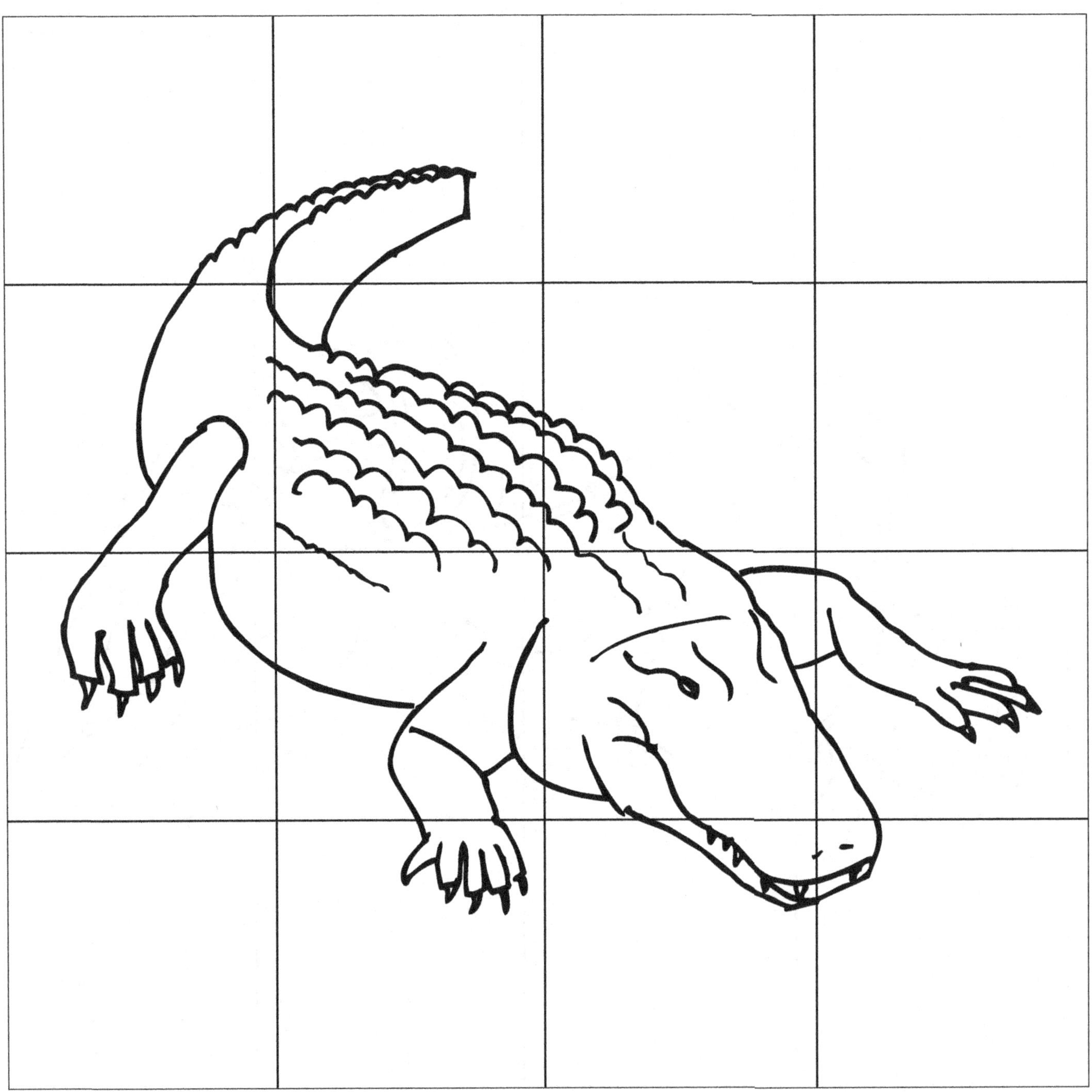

Alligator

Fox

Fox

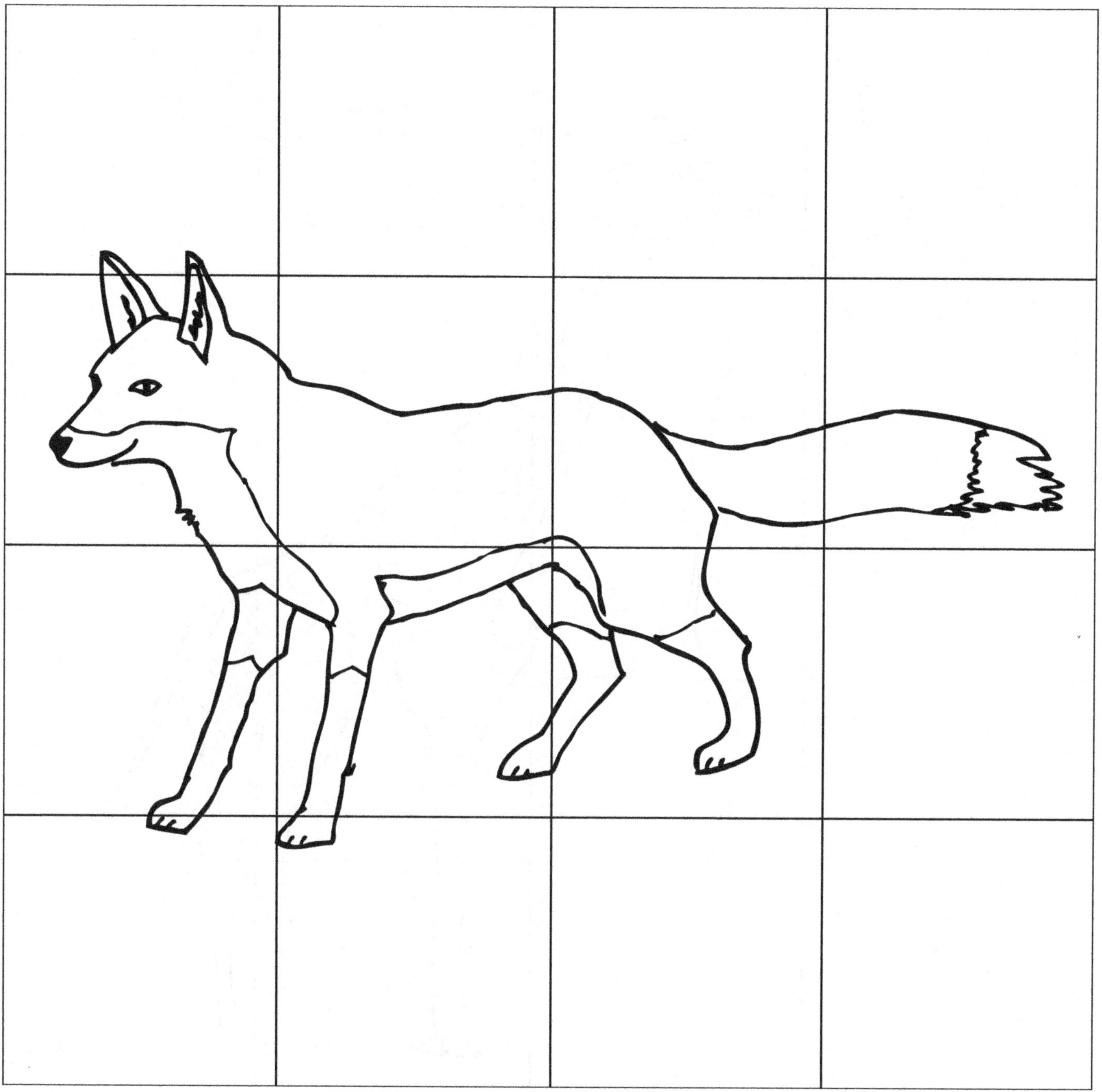

Giraffe

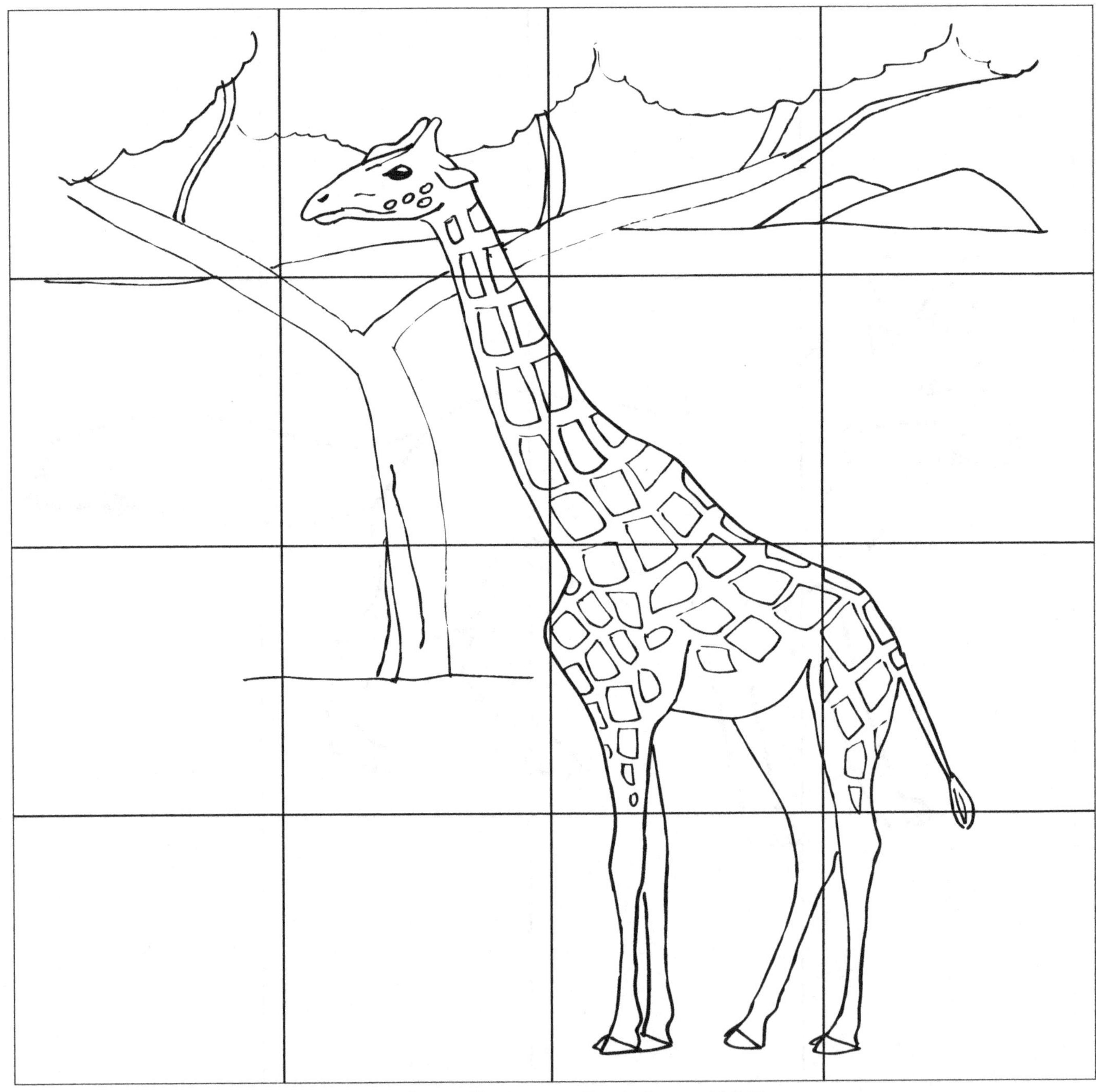

Giraffe

Bottlenose Dolphin

Bottlenose Dolphin

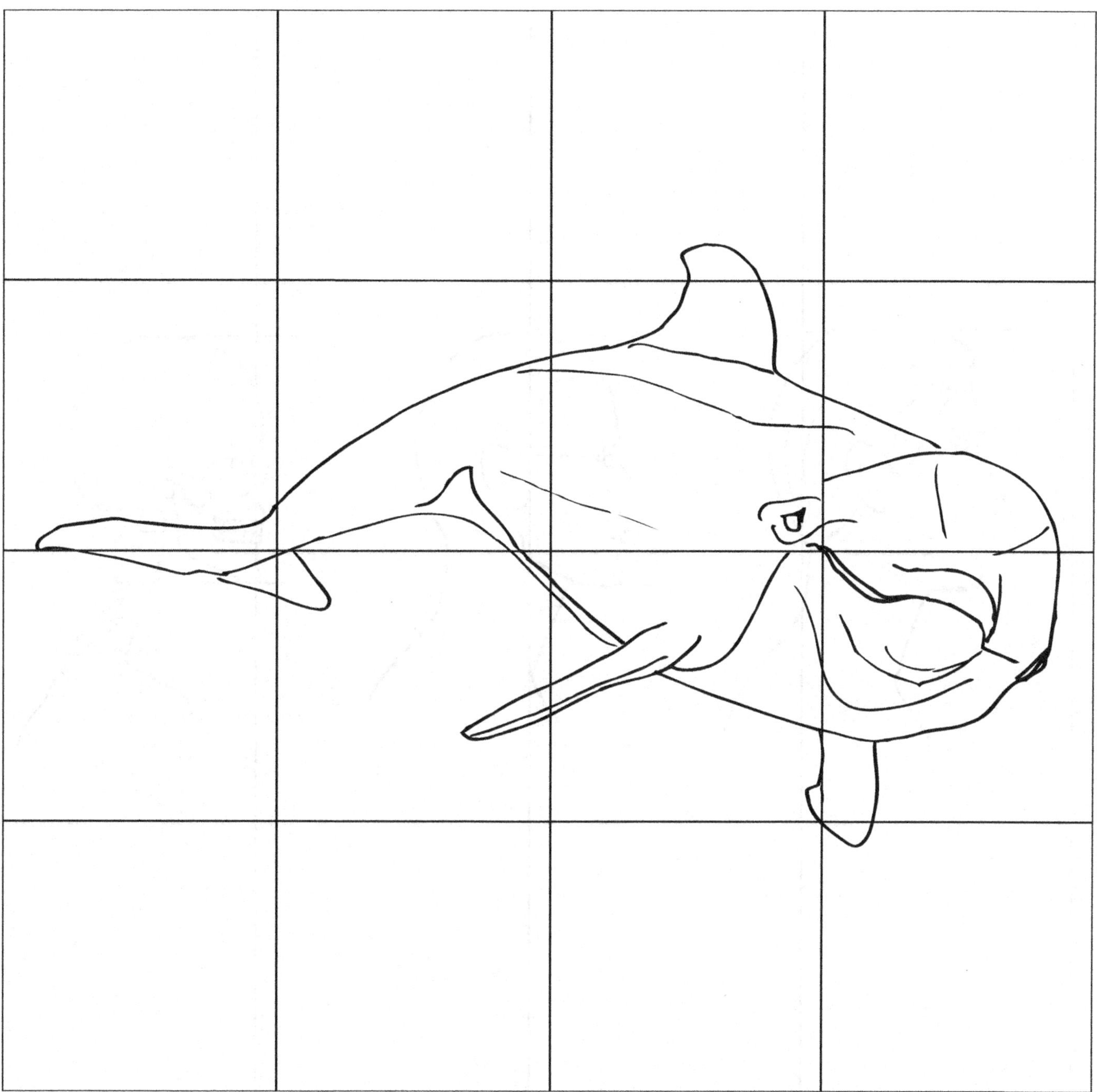

Man's Head

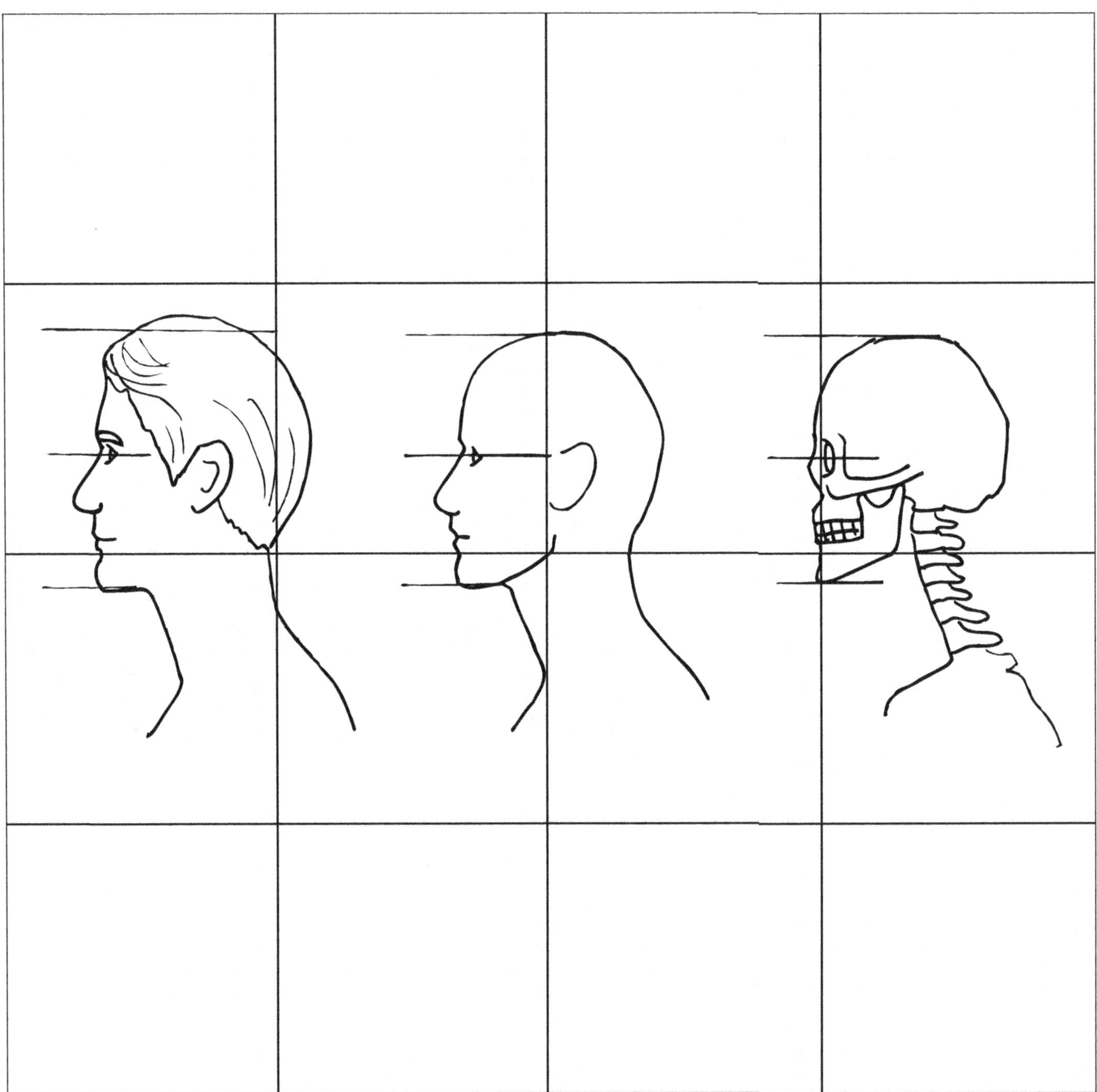

Man's Head

Chair

Chair

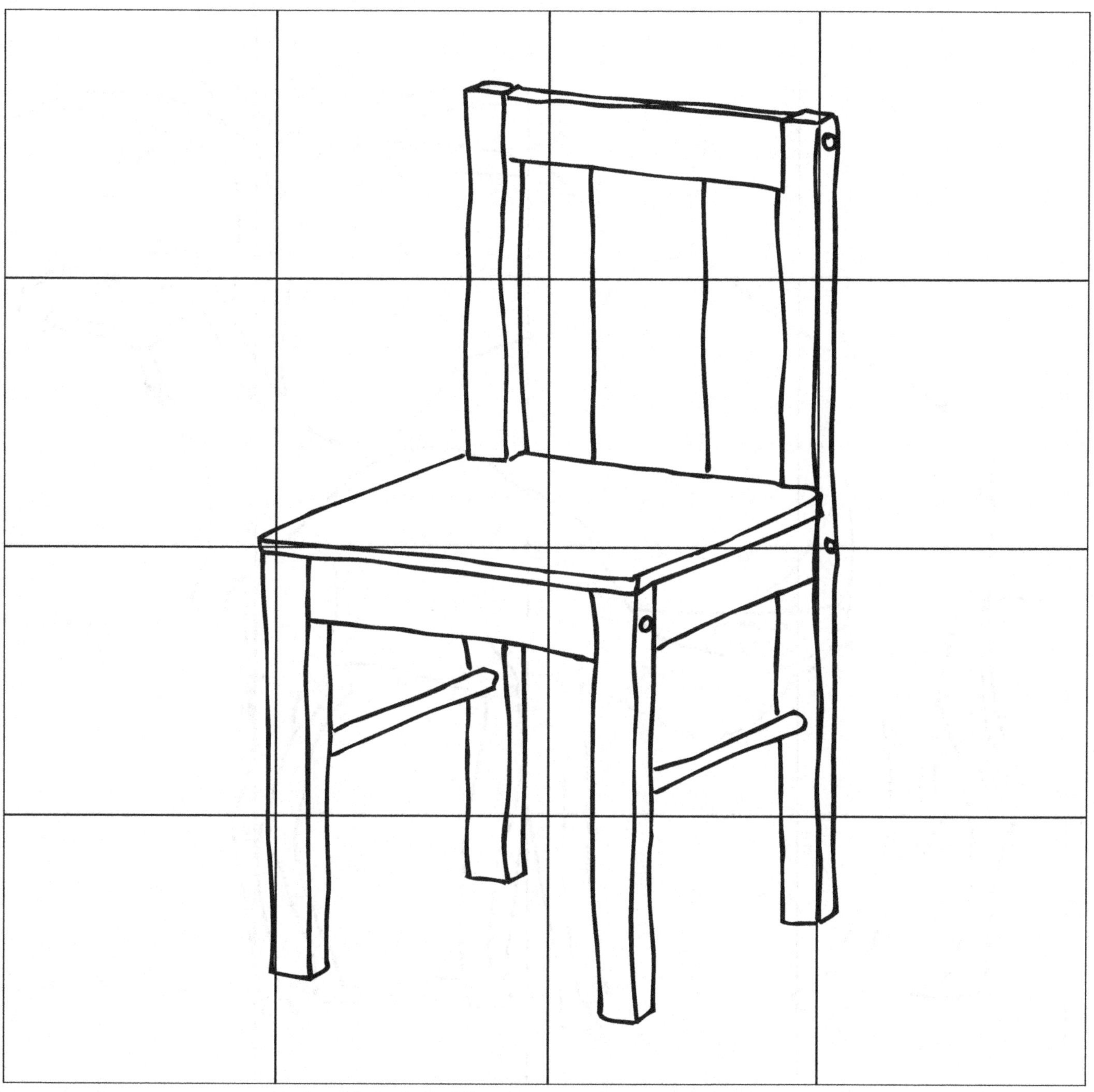

Arabian Camel and Calf

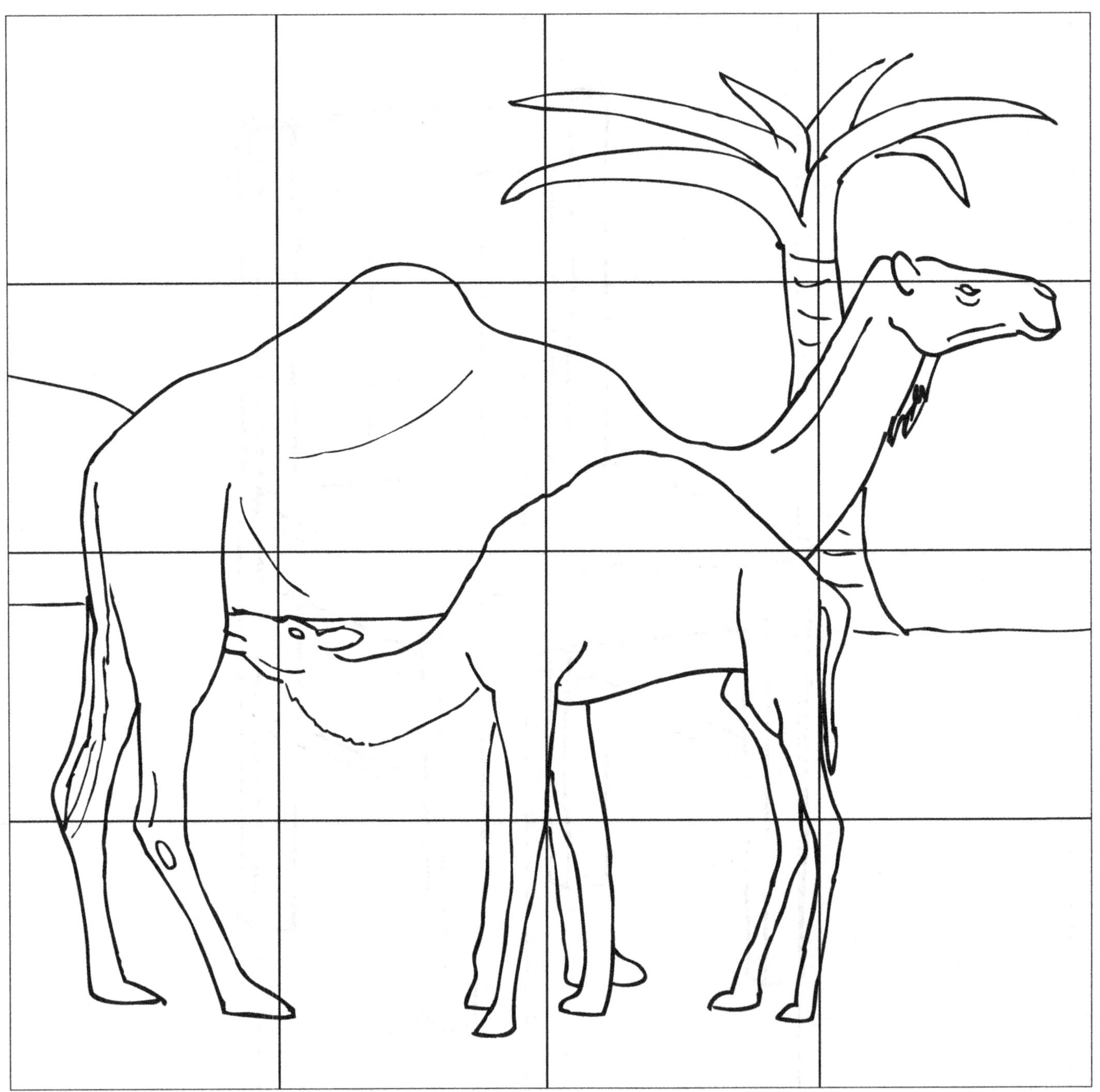

Arabian Camel and Calf

Thirsty Cockatoo

<table>
<tr><td></td><td></td><td></td><td></td></tr>
<tr><td></td><td></td><td></td><td></td></tr>
<tr><td></td><td></td><td></td><td></td></tr>
<tr><td></td><td></td><td></td><td></td></tr>
</table>

Thirsty Cockatoo

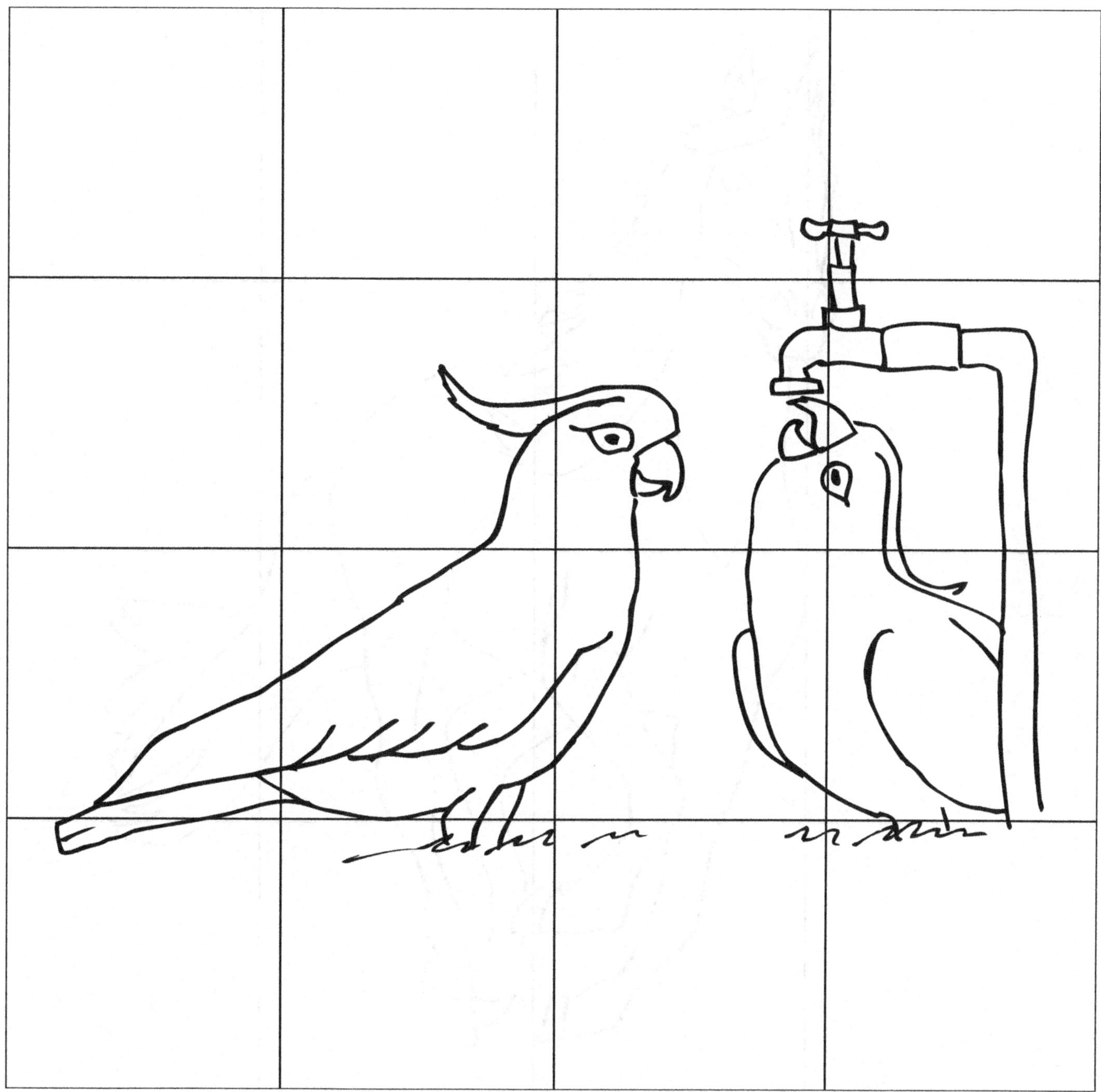

Horse on the Beach

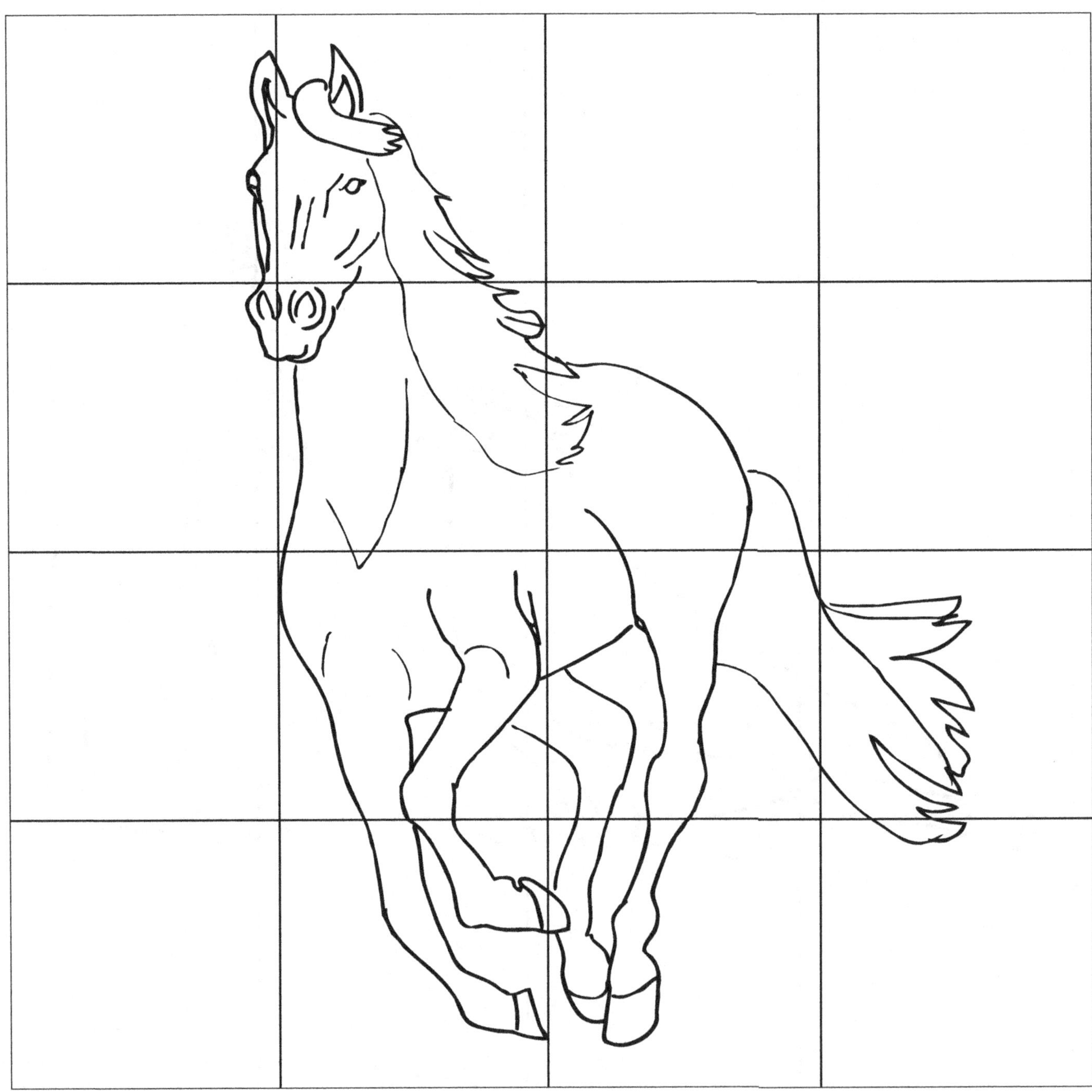

Horse on the Beach

Walking the Dog

Walking the Dog

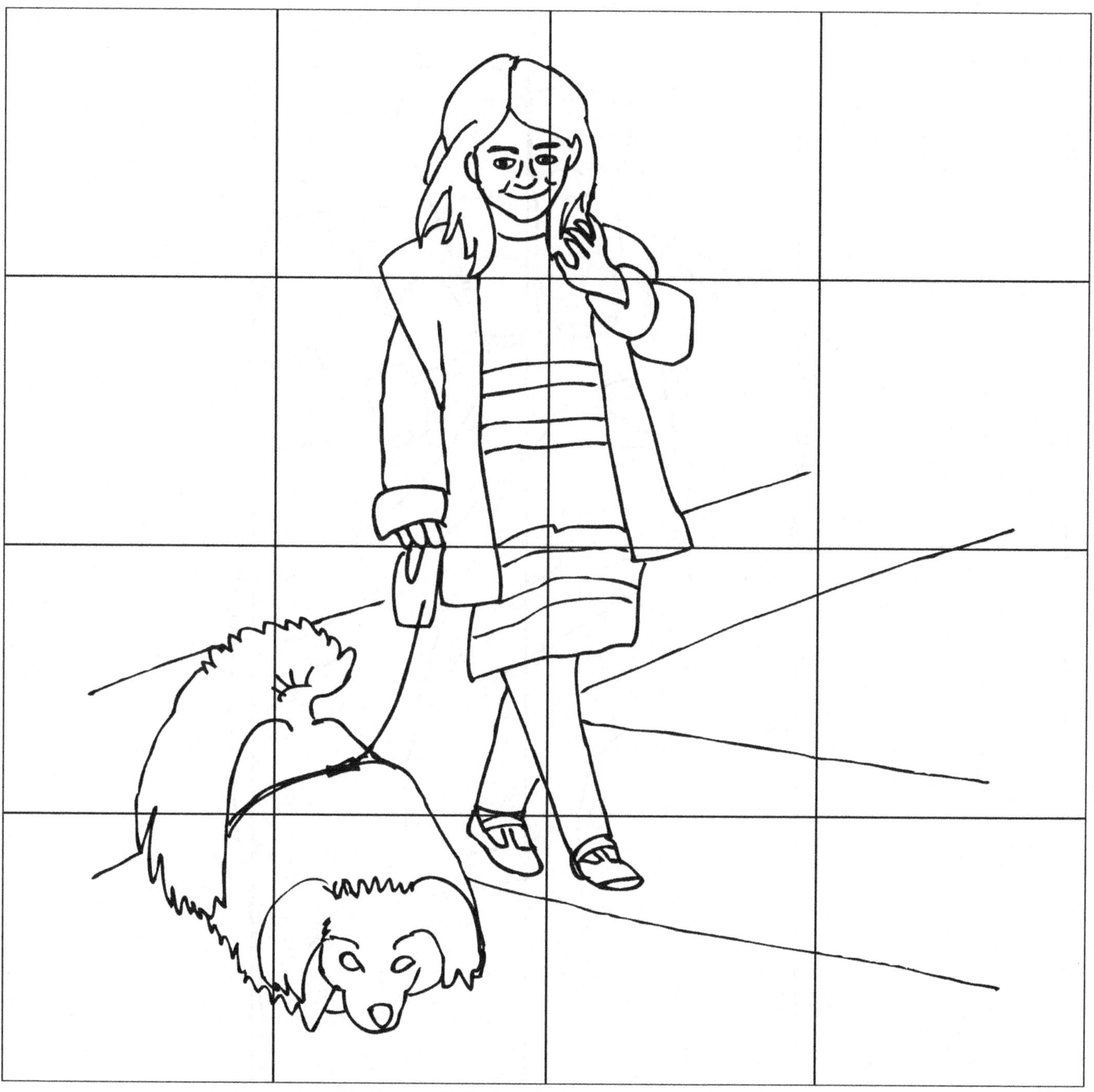

Left Hand

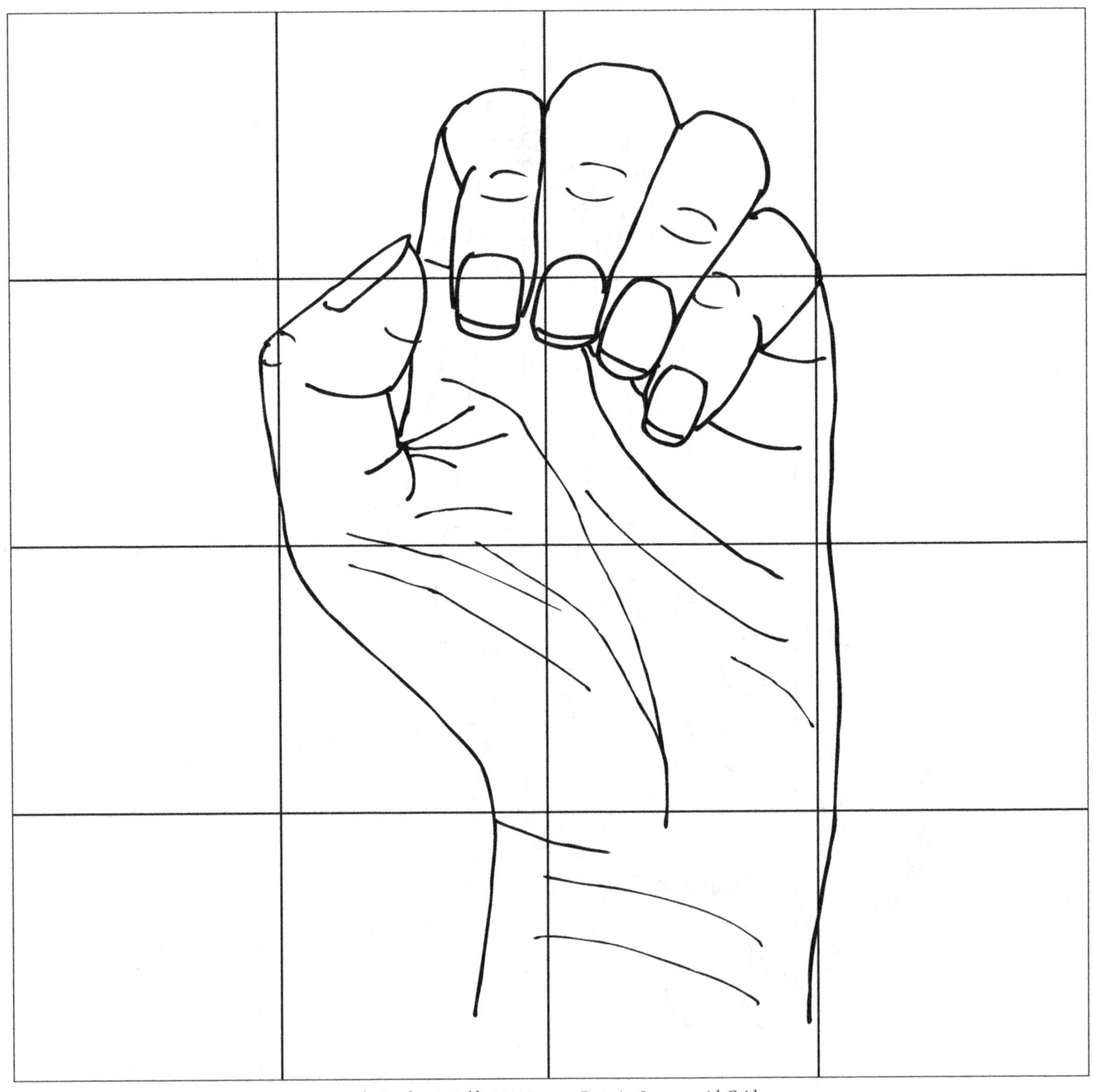

Left Hand

Piglet

Piglet

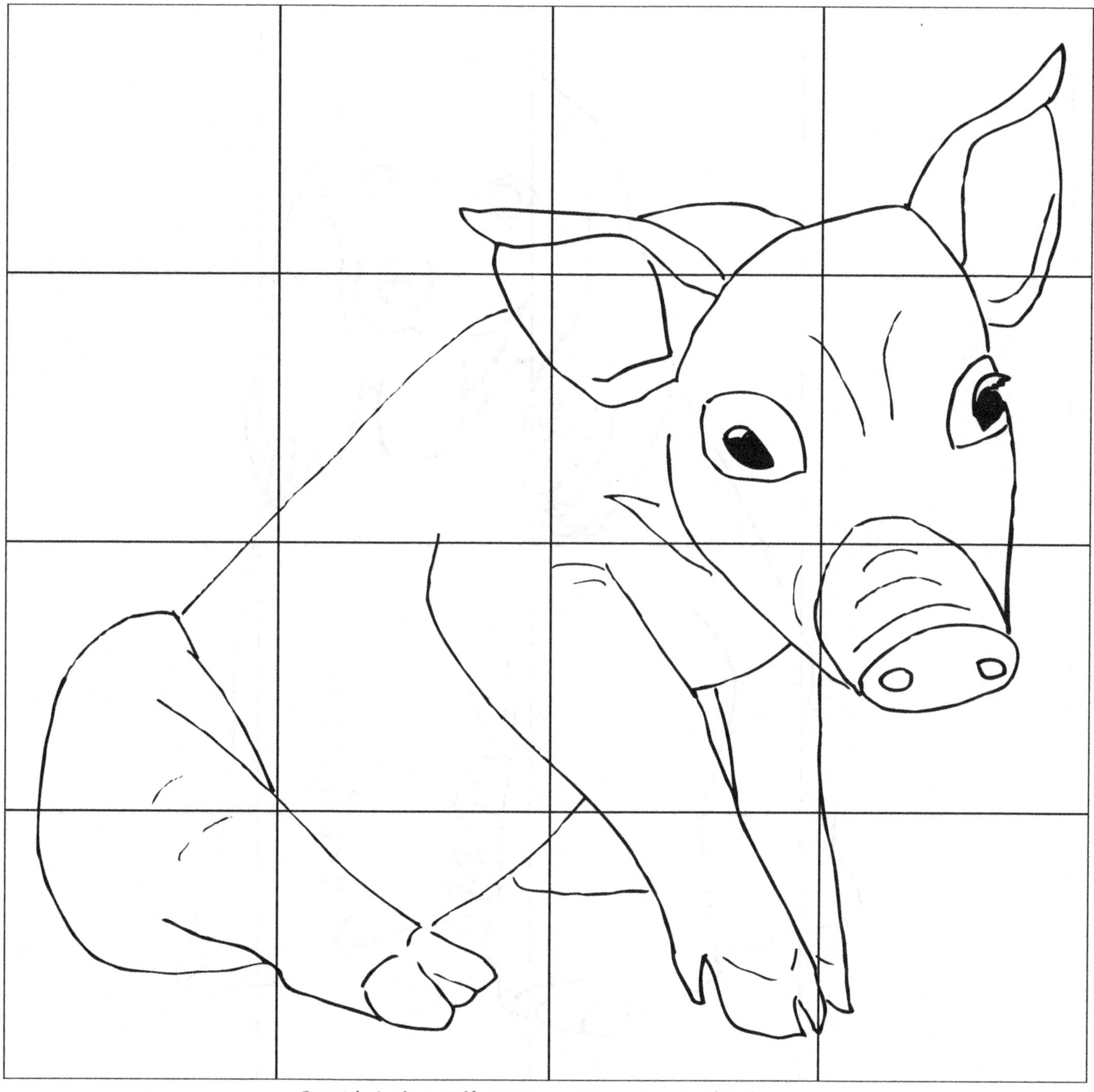

Cocker Spaniel

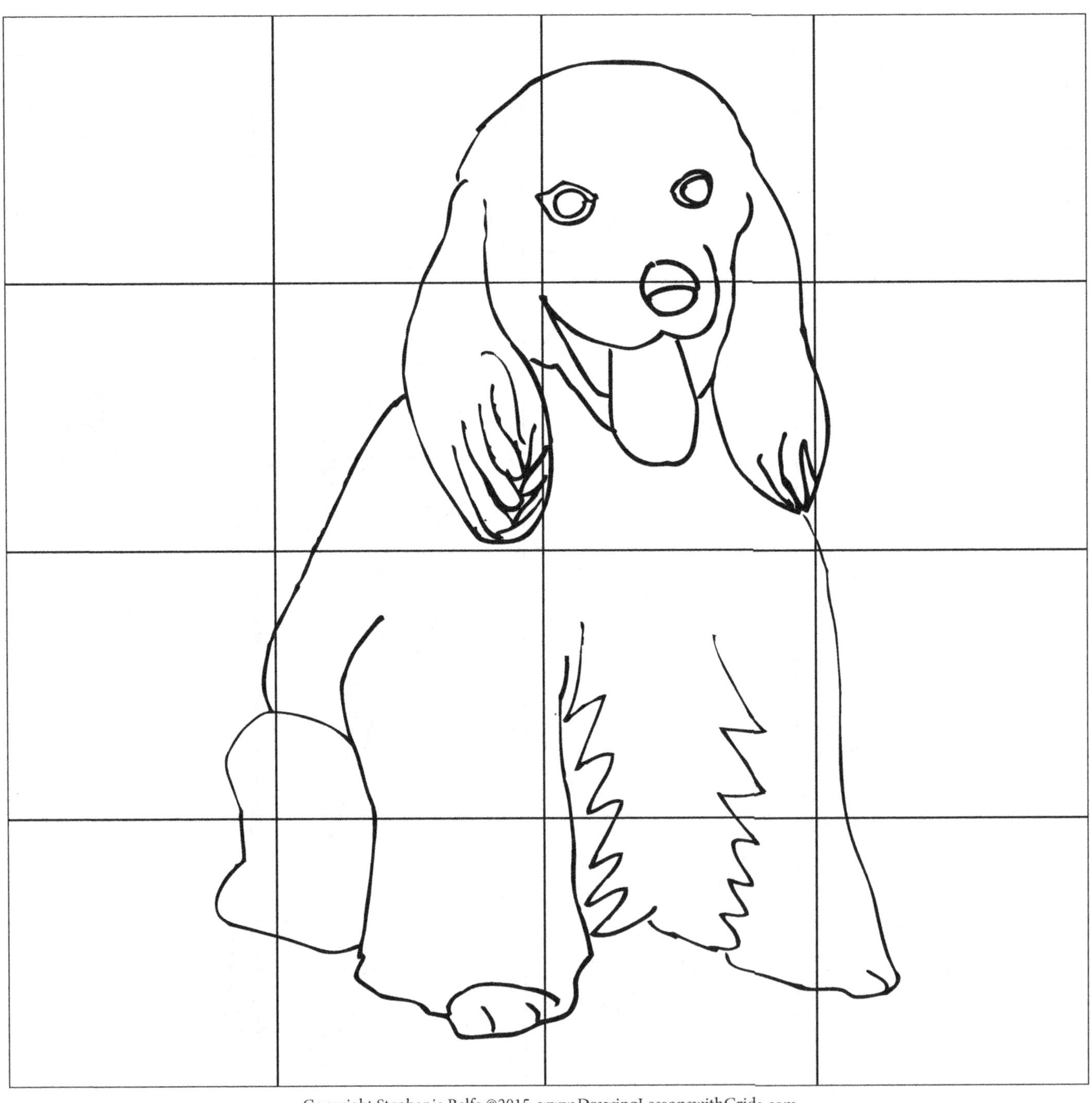

Cocker Spaniel

House

House

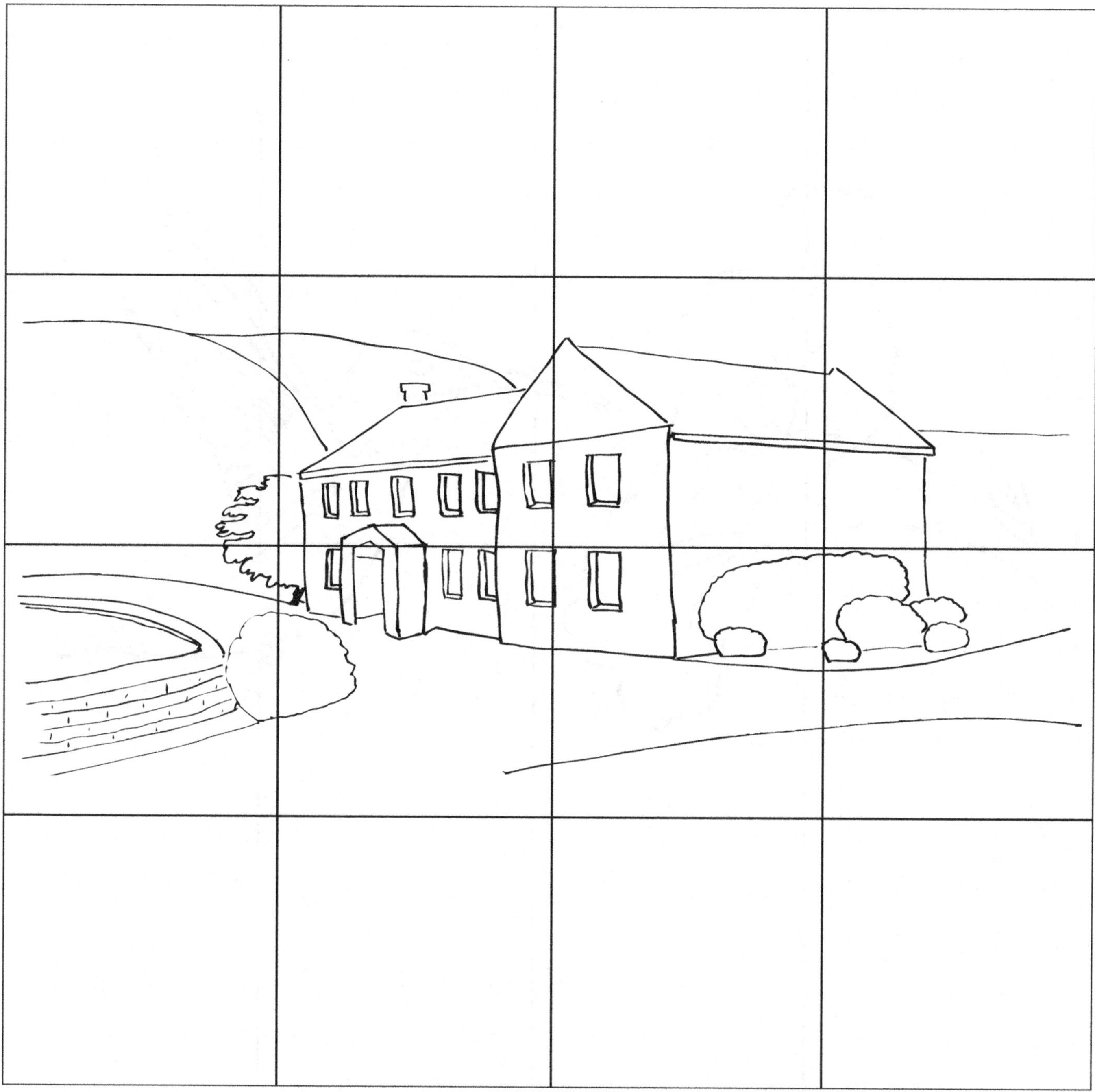

Hummingbird

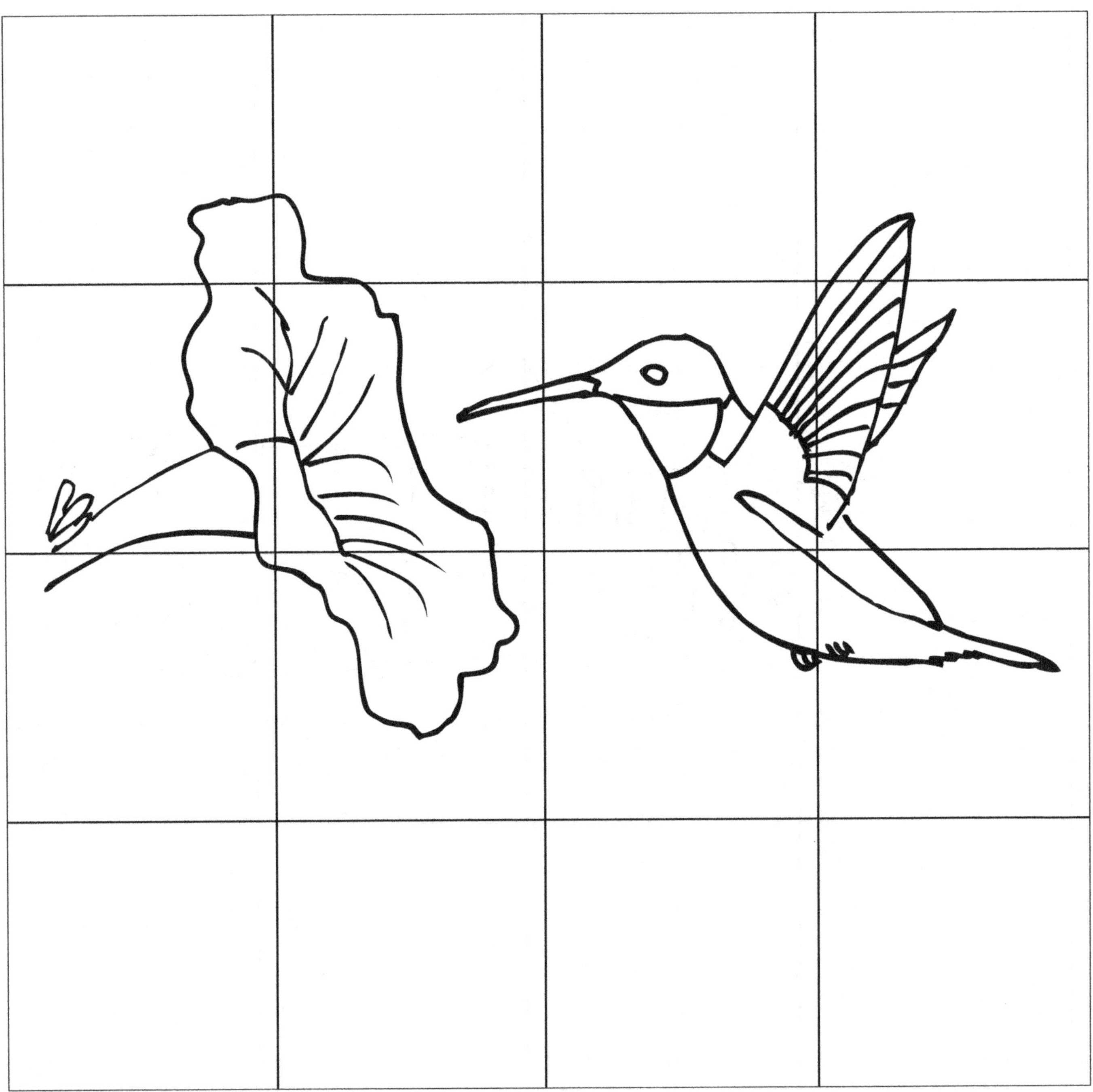

Hummingbird

Kangaroo and Joey

Kangaroo and Joey

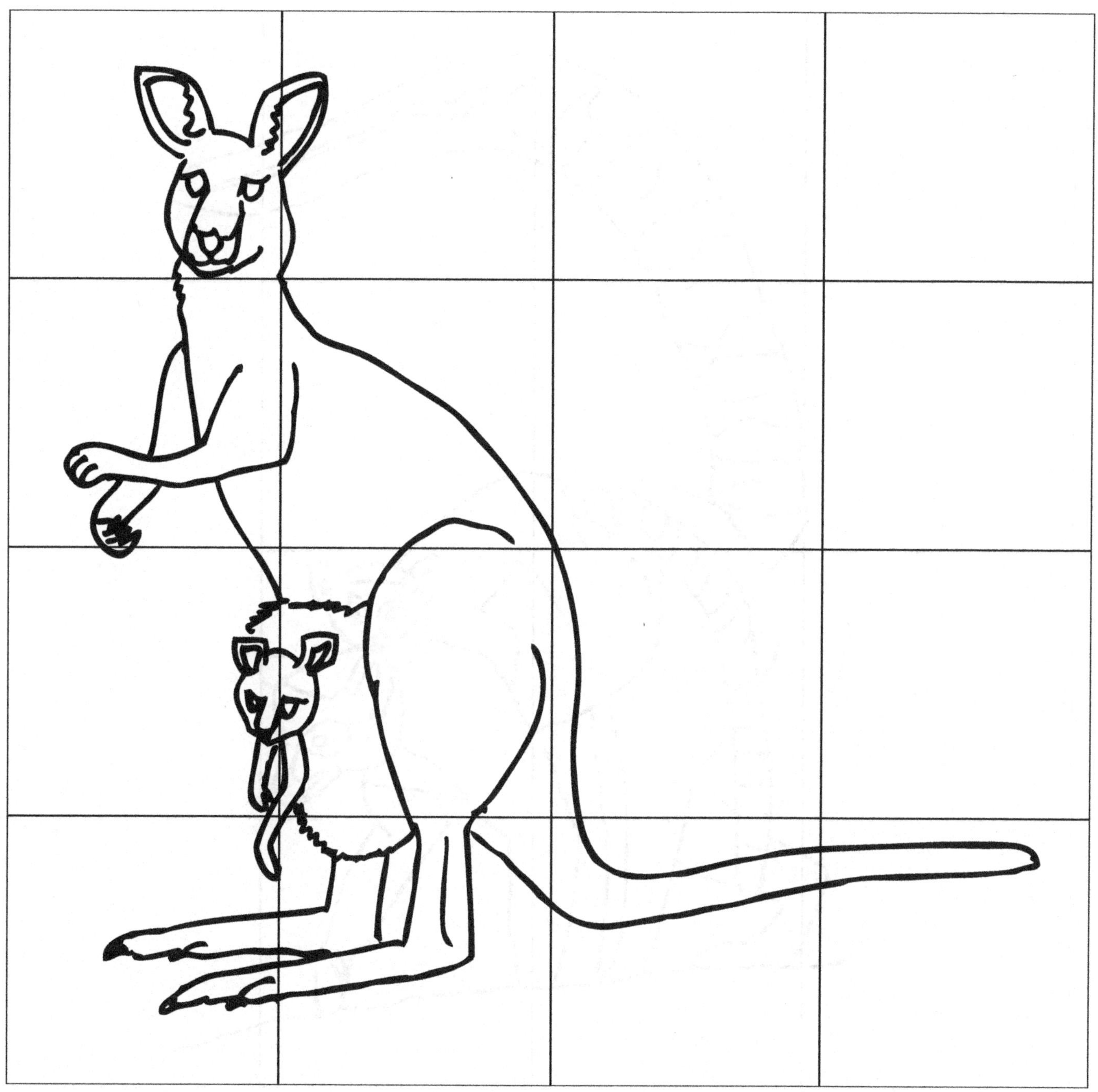

Ring-Tailed Lemur and Baby

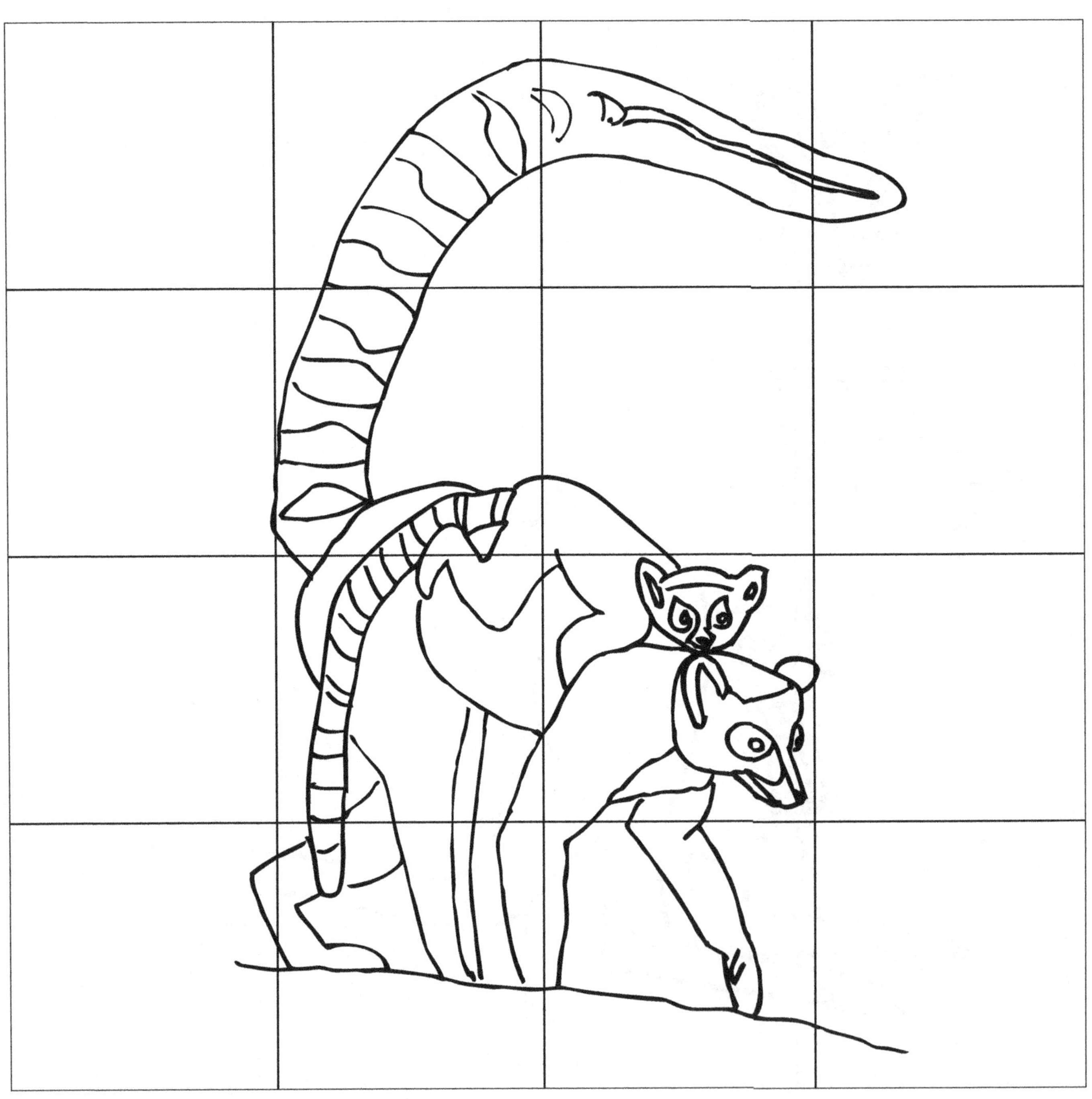

Ring-Tailed Lemur and Baby

Western Riding Style

Western Riding Style

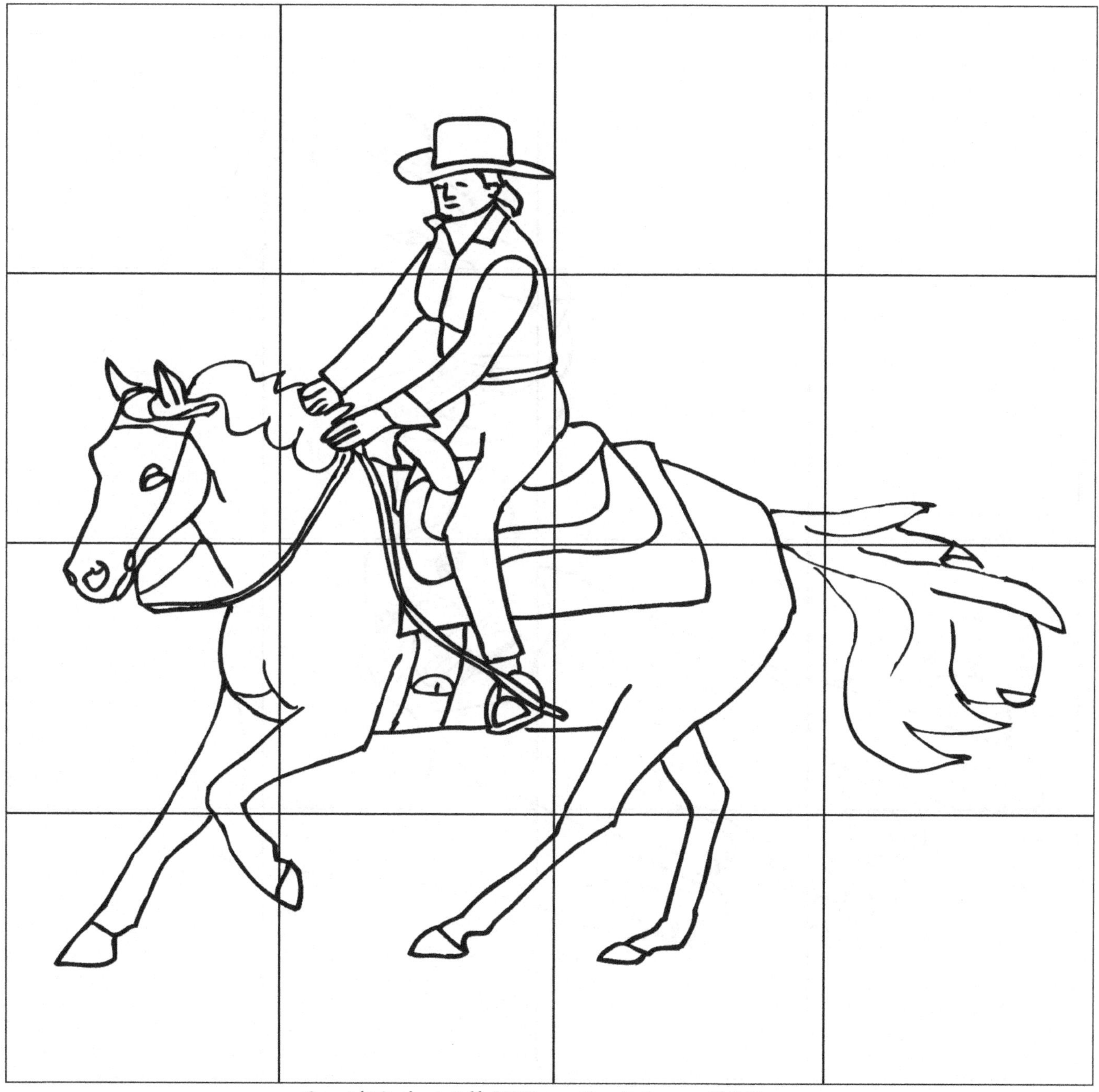

Lioness and Cub

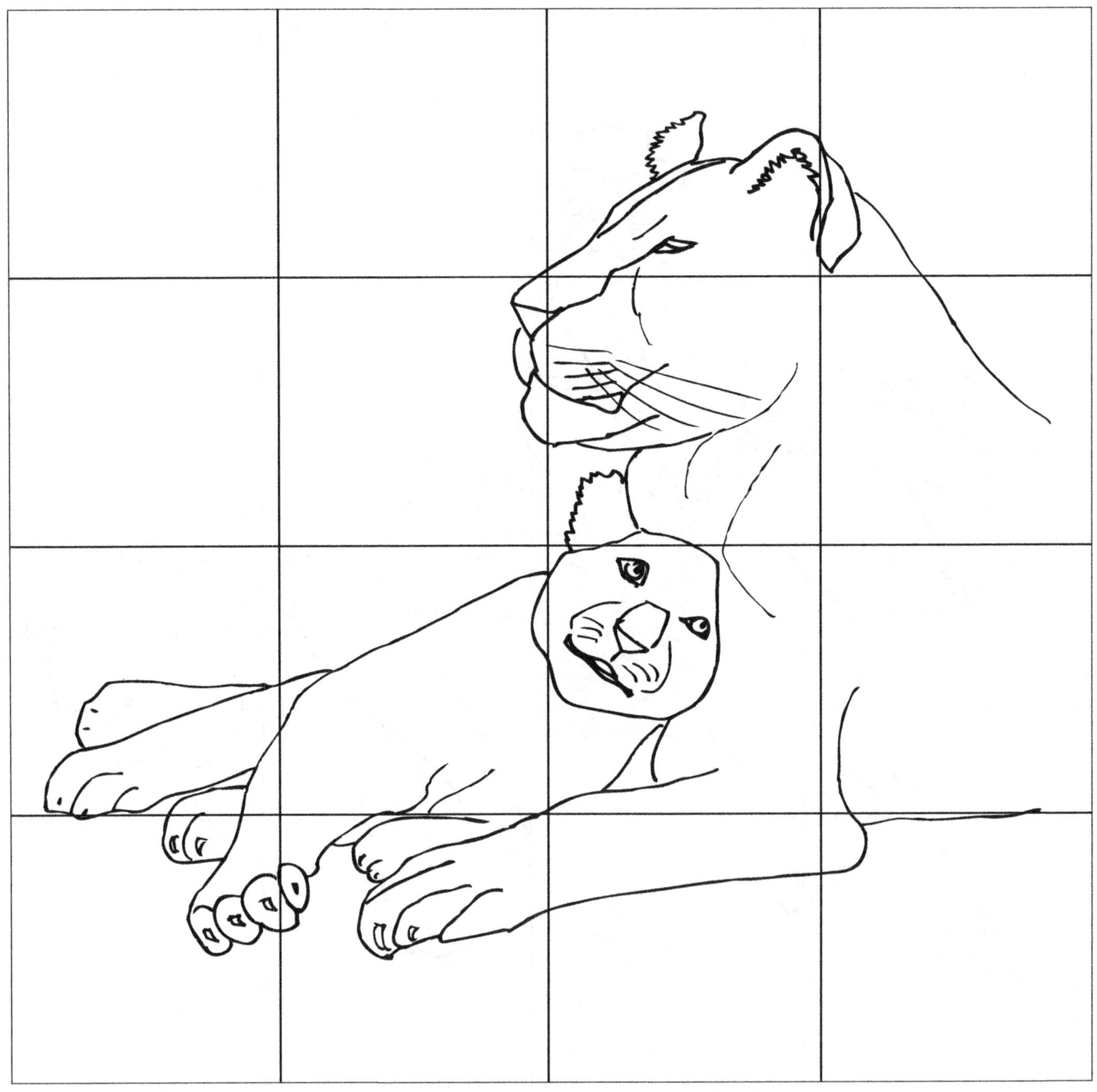

Lioness and Cub

Caracal

Caracal

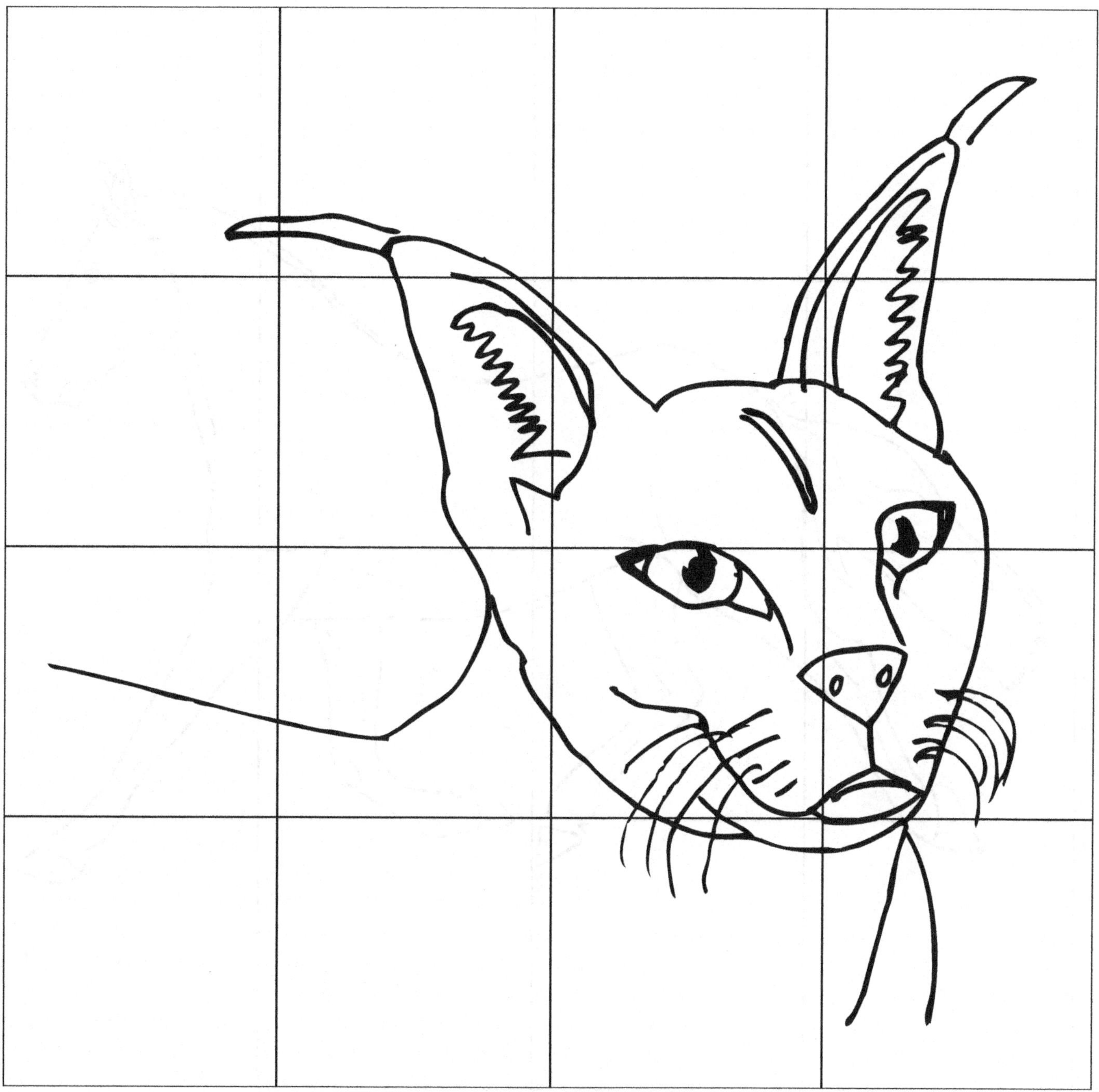

Horse Trotting

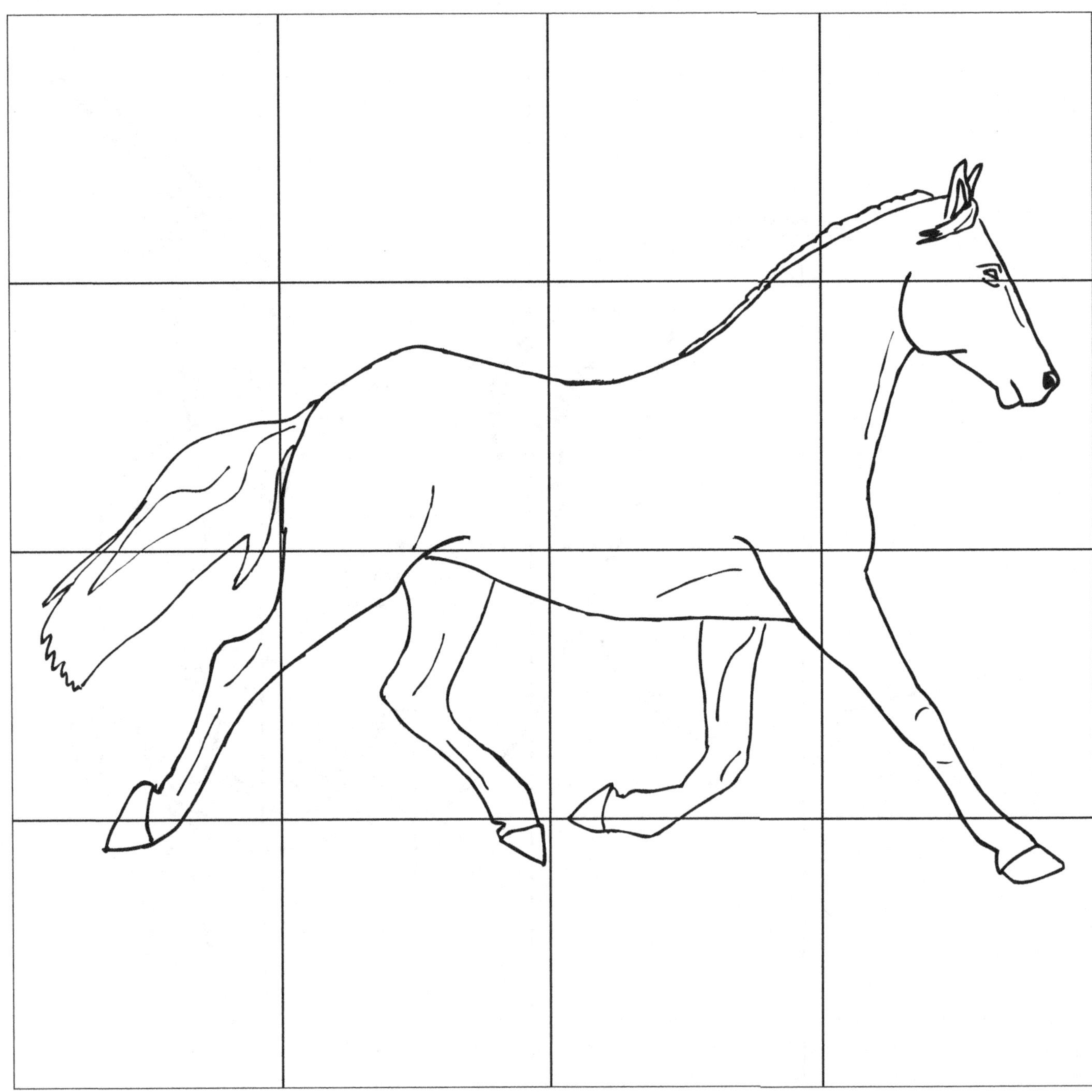

Horse Trotting

Rose

Rose

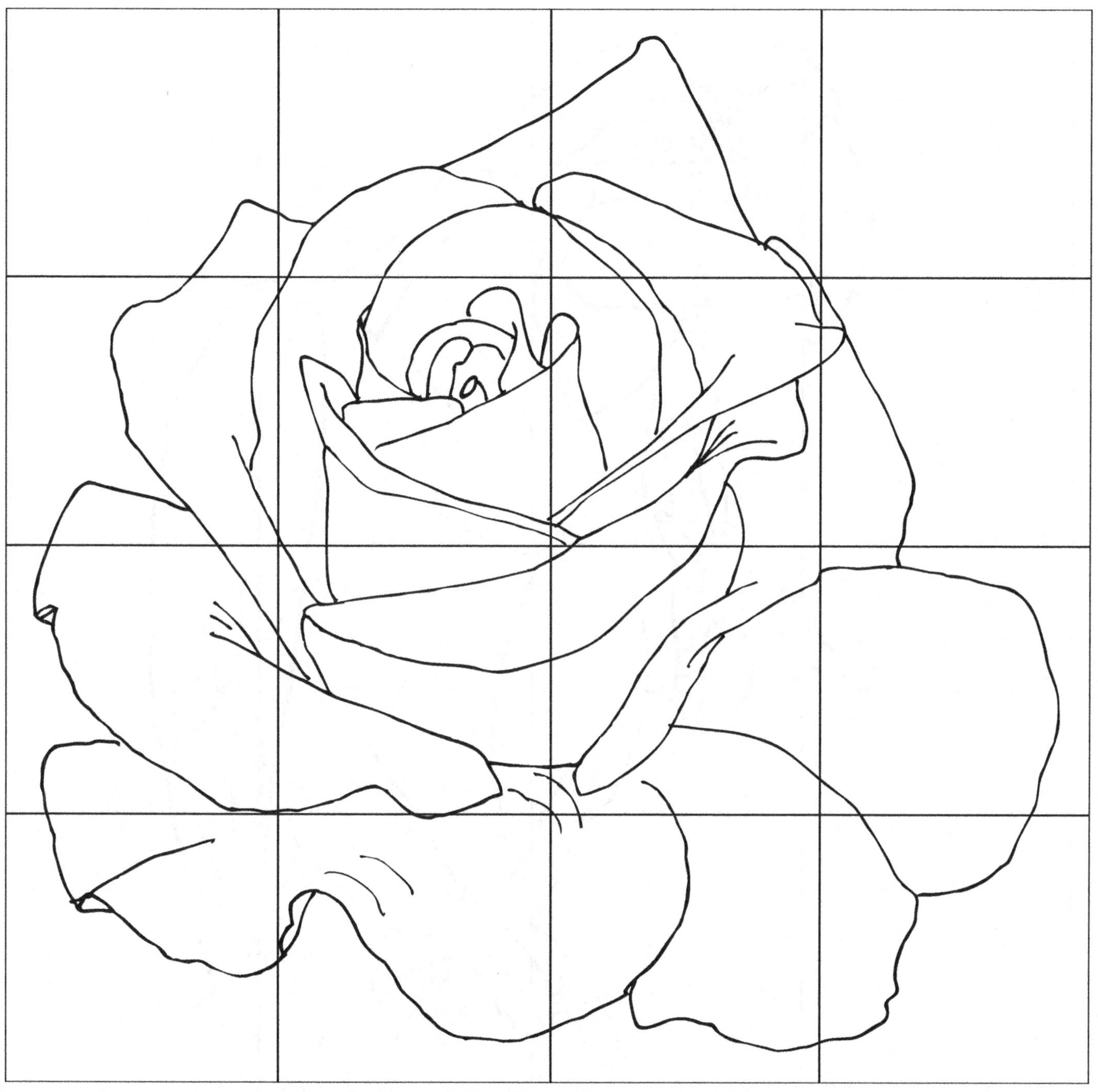

Blue Macaw

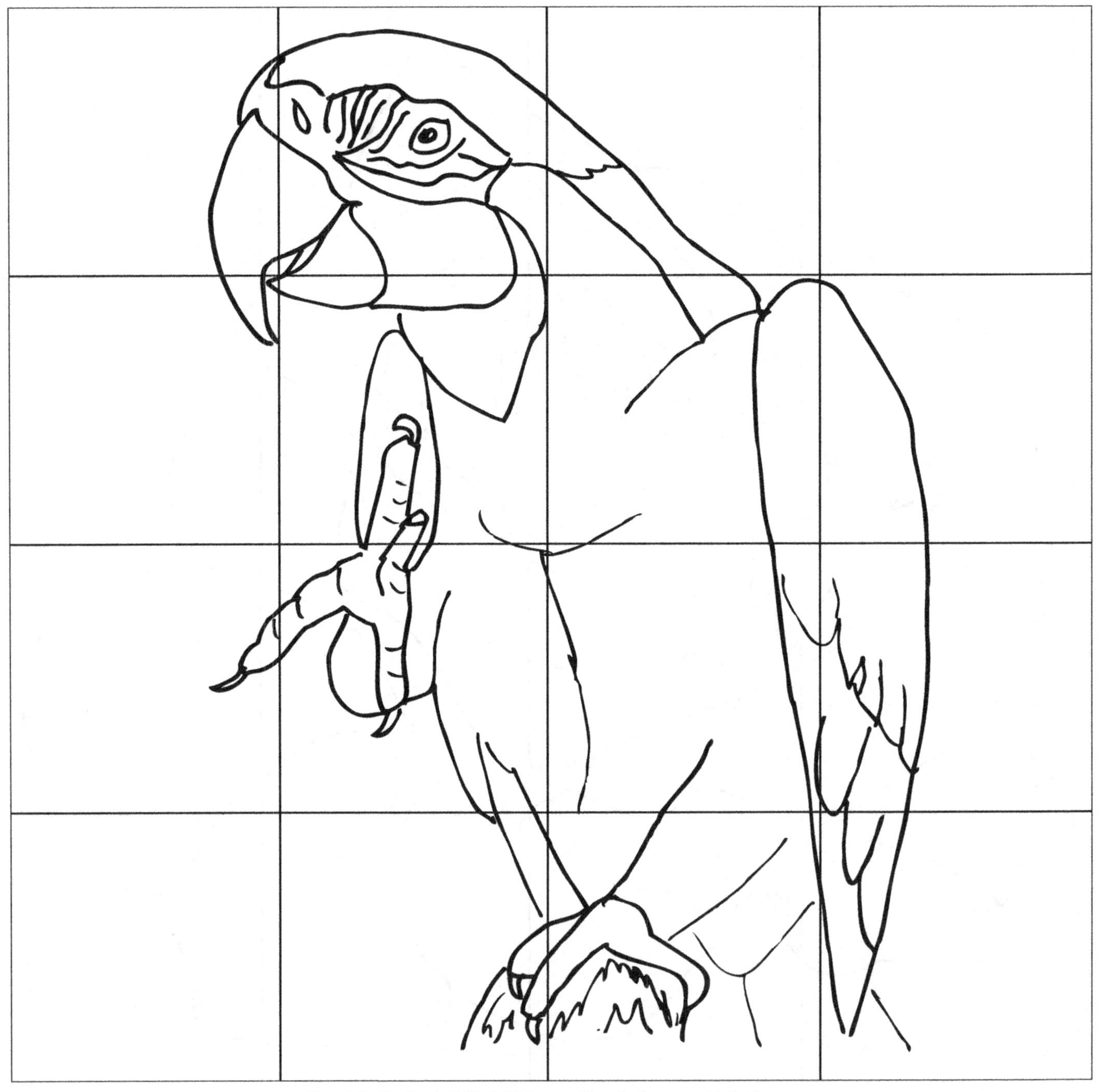

Blue Macaw

Humpback Whale and Calf

Humpback Whale and Calf

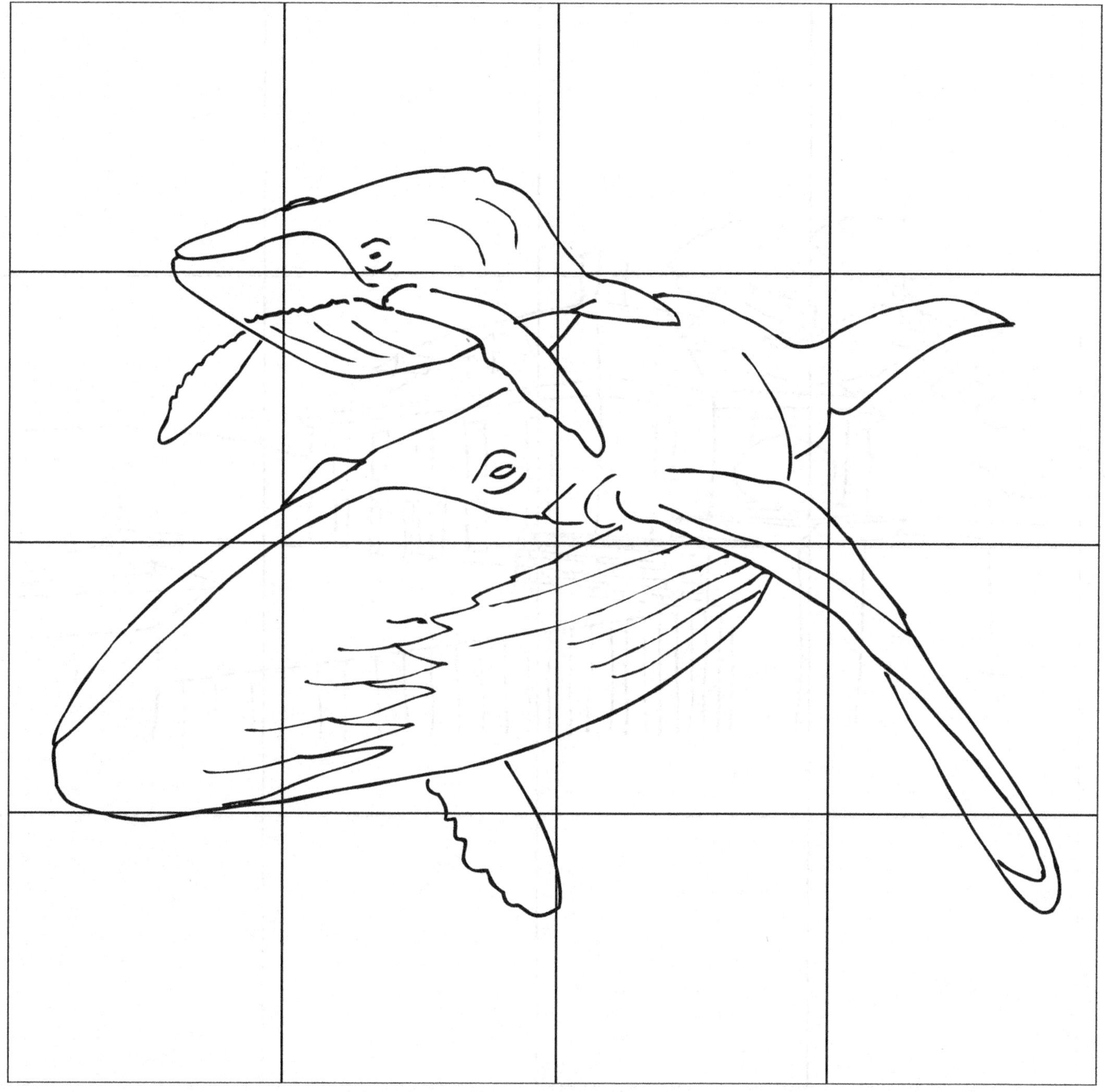

Mansion

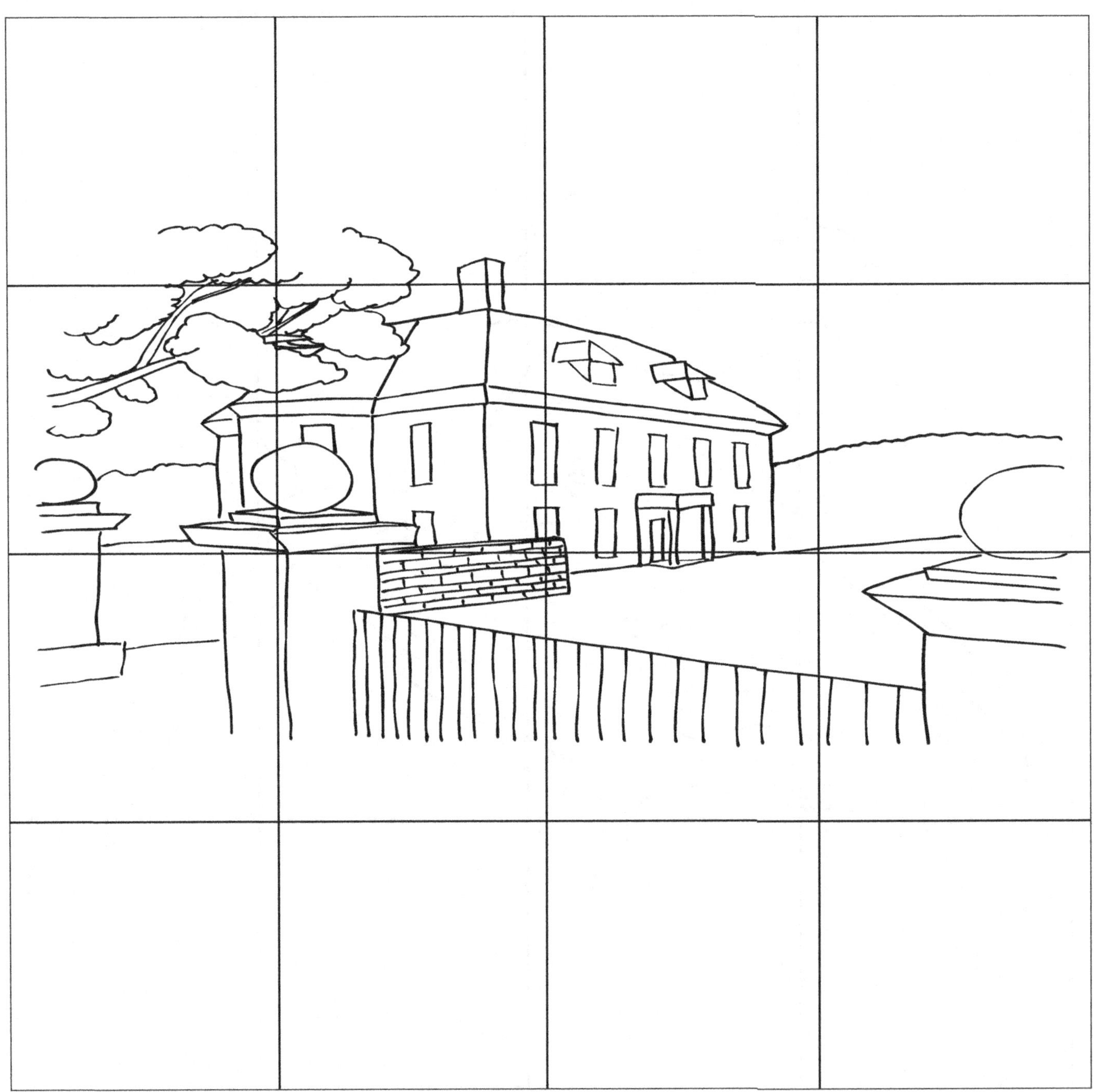

Mansion

Okapi

Okapi

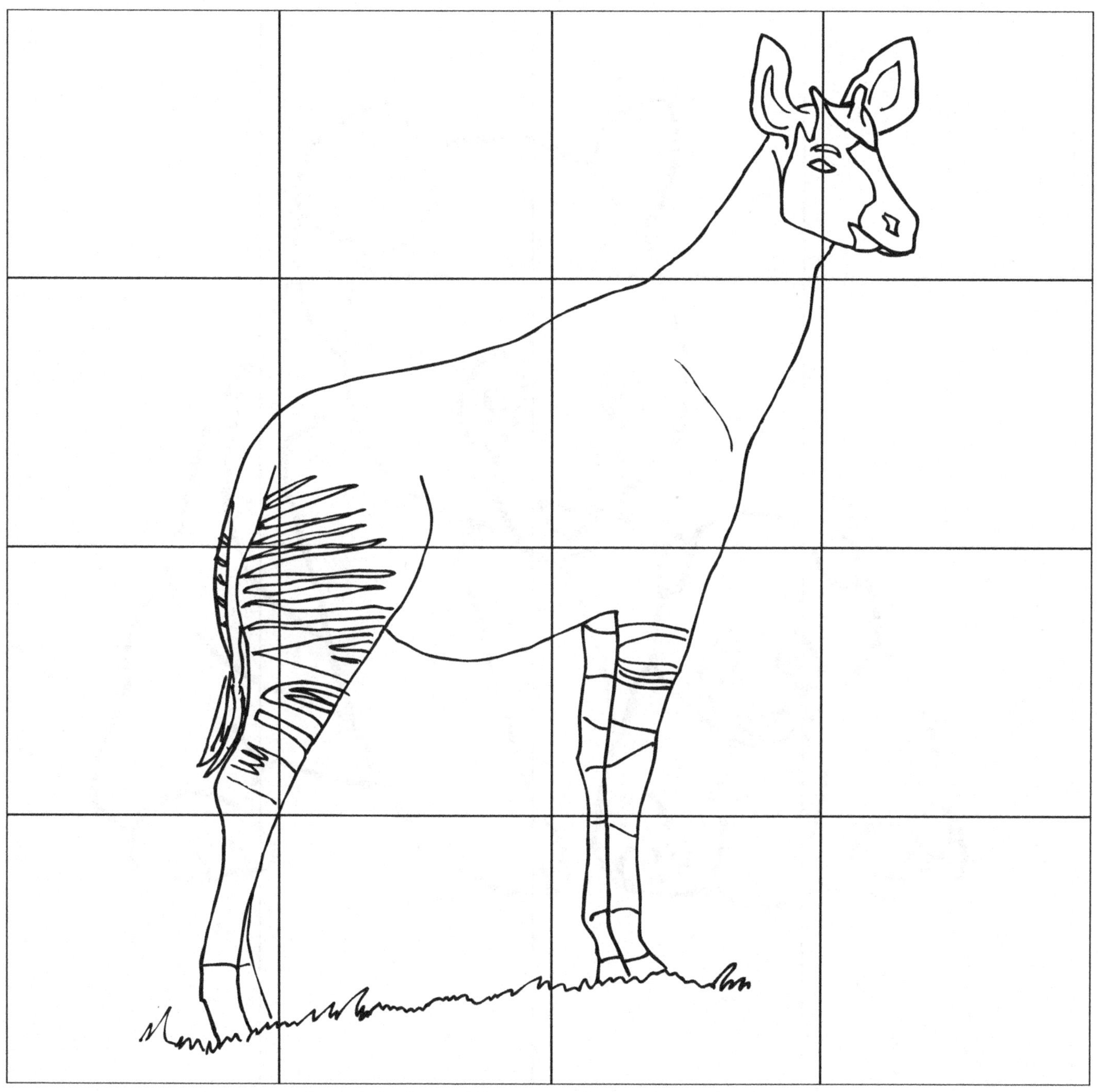

Panda and Cub

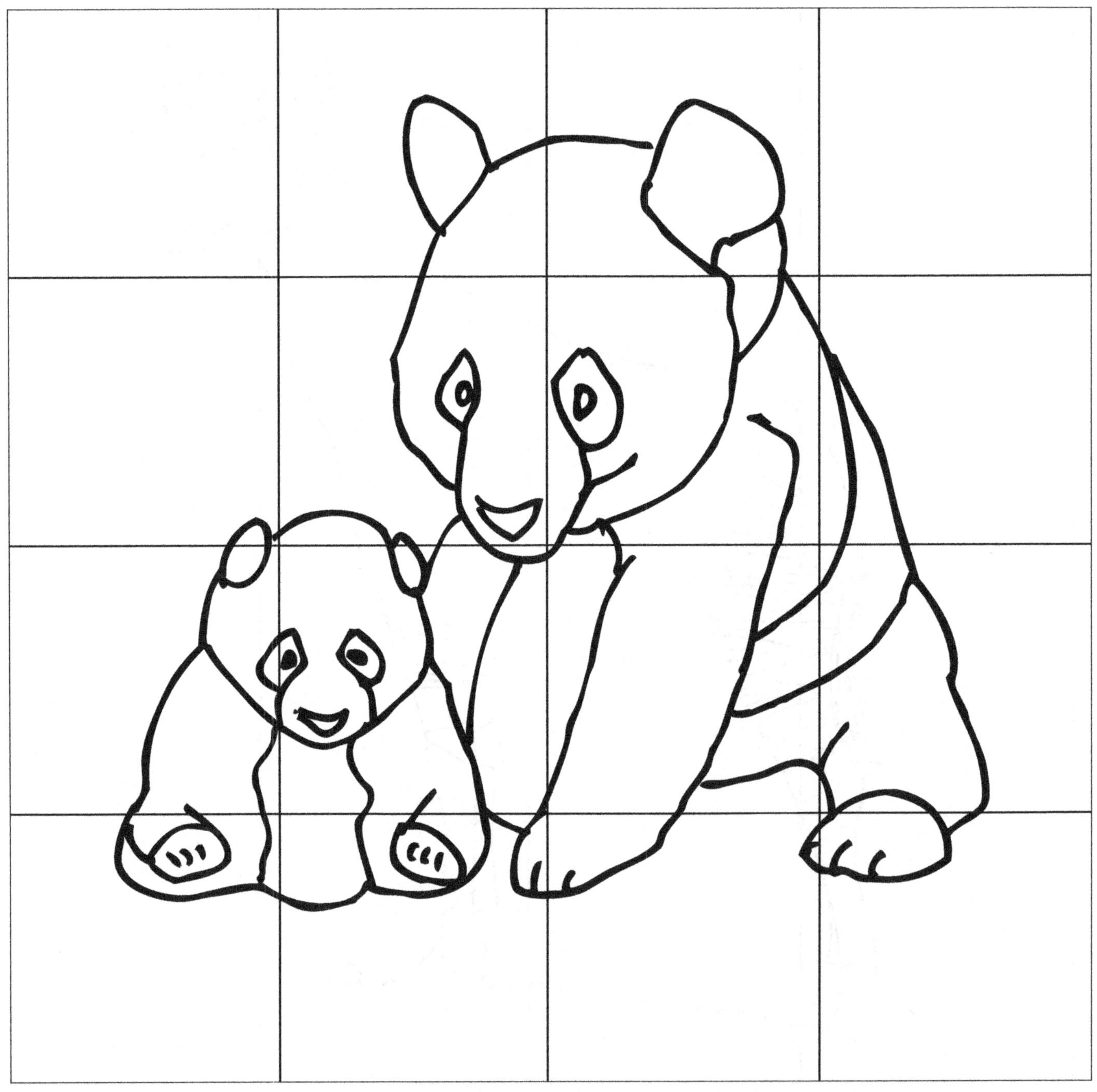

Panda and Cub

White Tailed Buck

White Tailed Buck

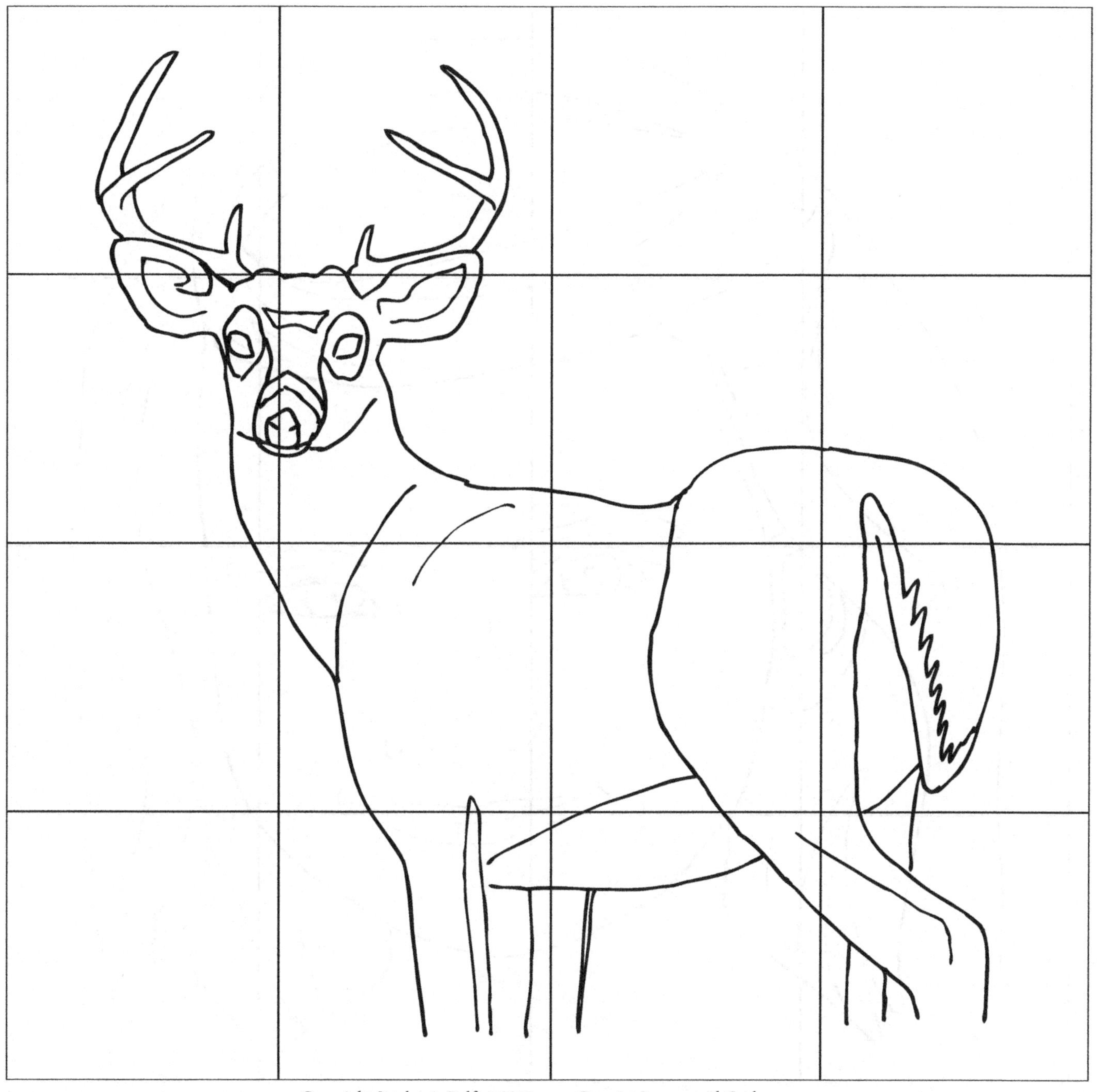

Young Lady

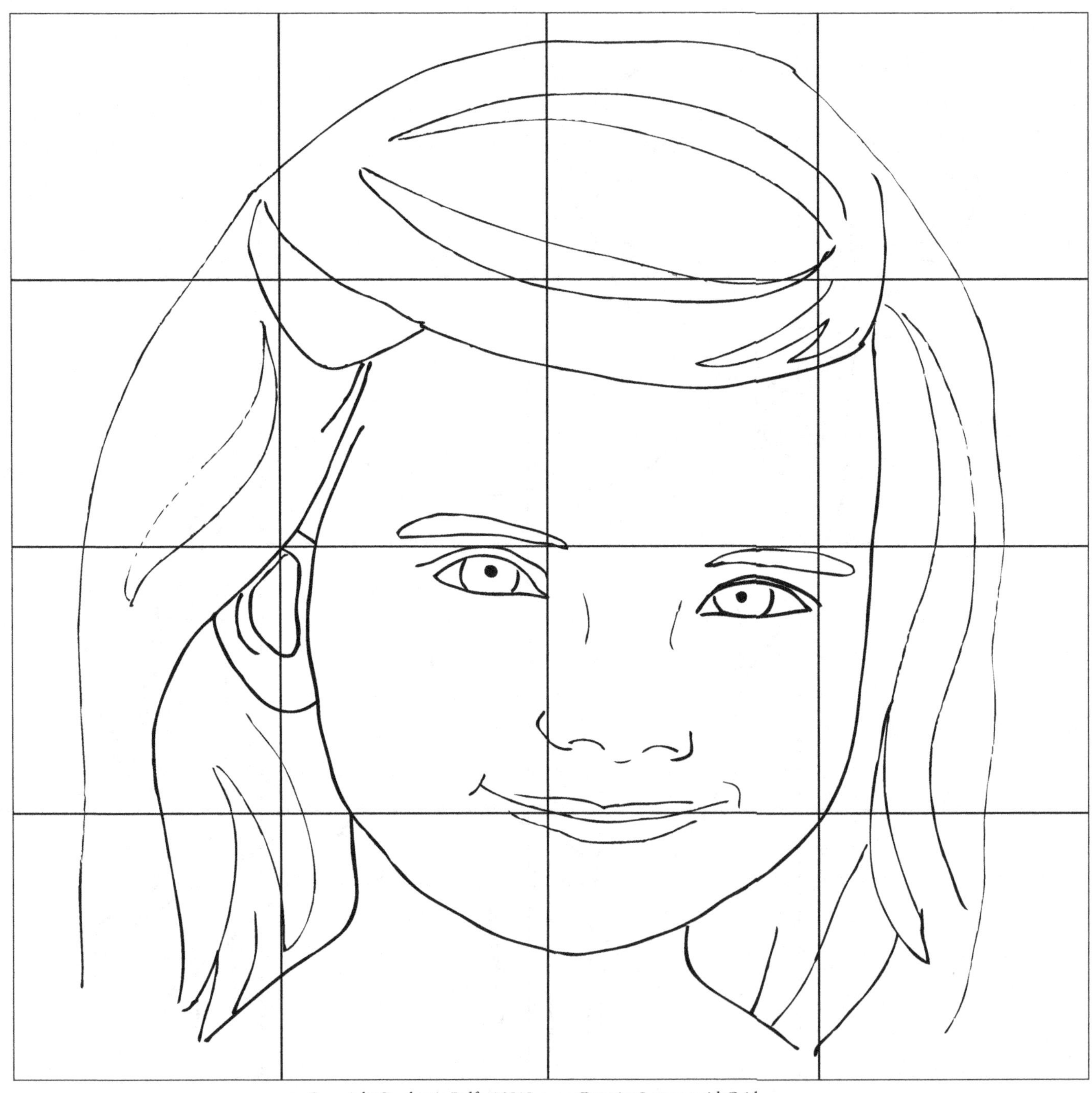

Young Lady

Humboldt Penguin

Humboldt Penguin

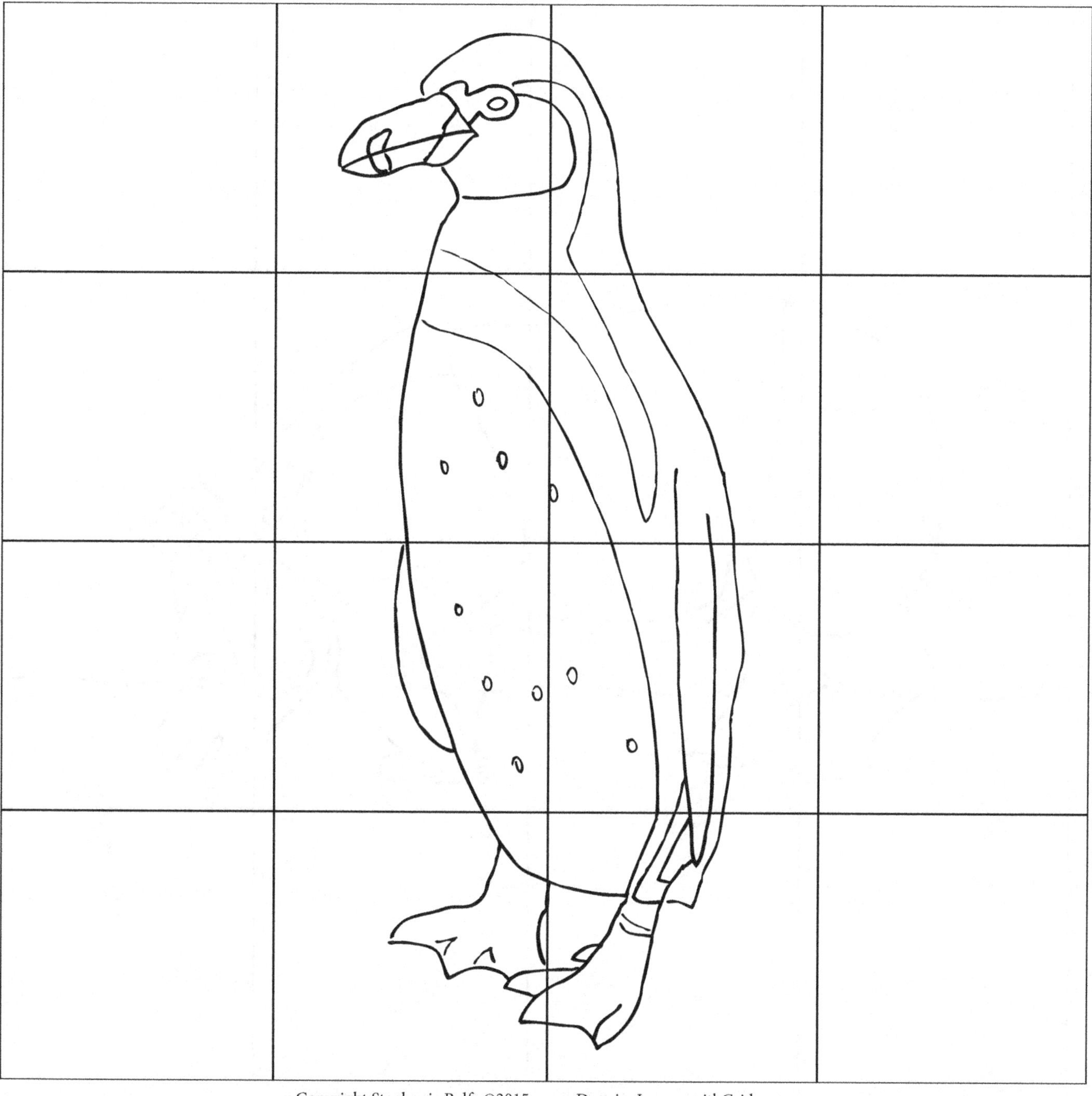

Indian Rhino

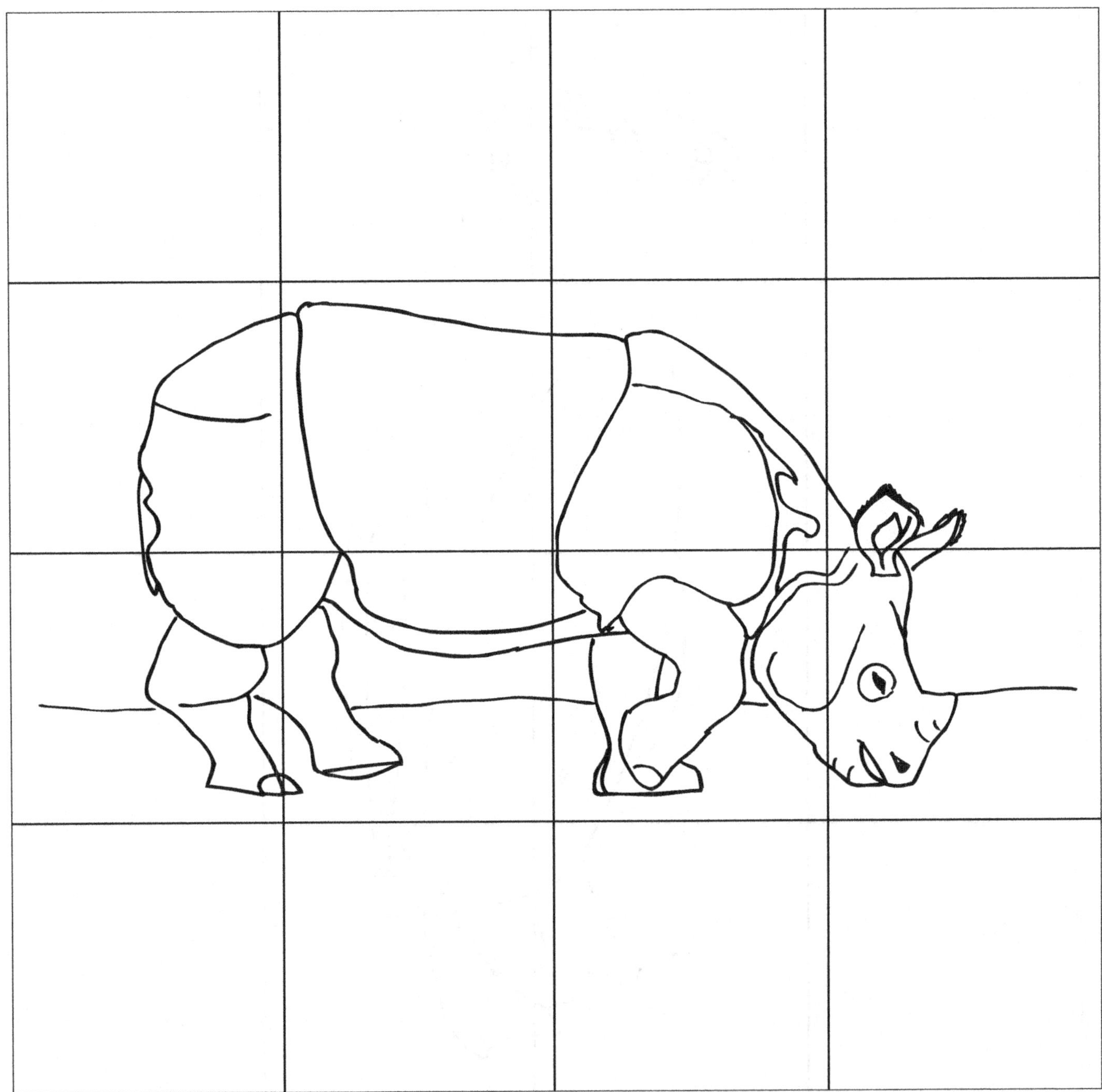

Indian Rhino

Ring Tailed Cat

Ring Tailed Cat

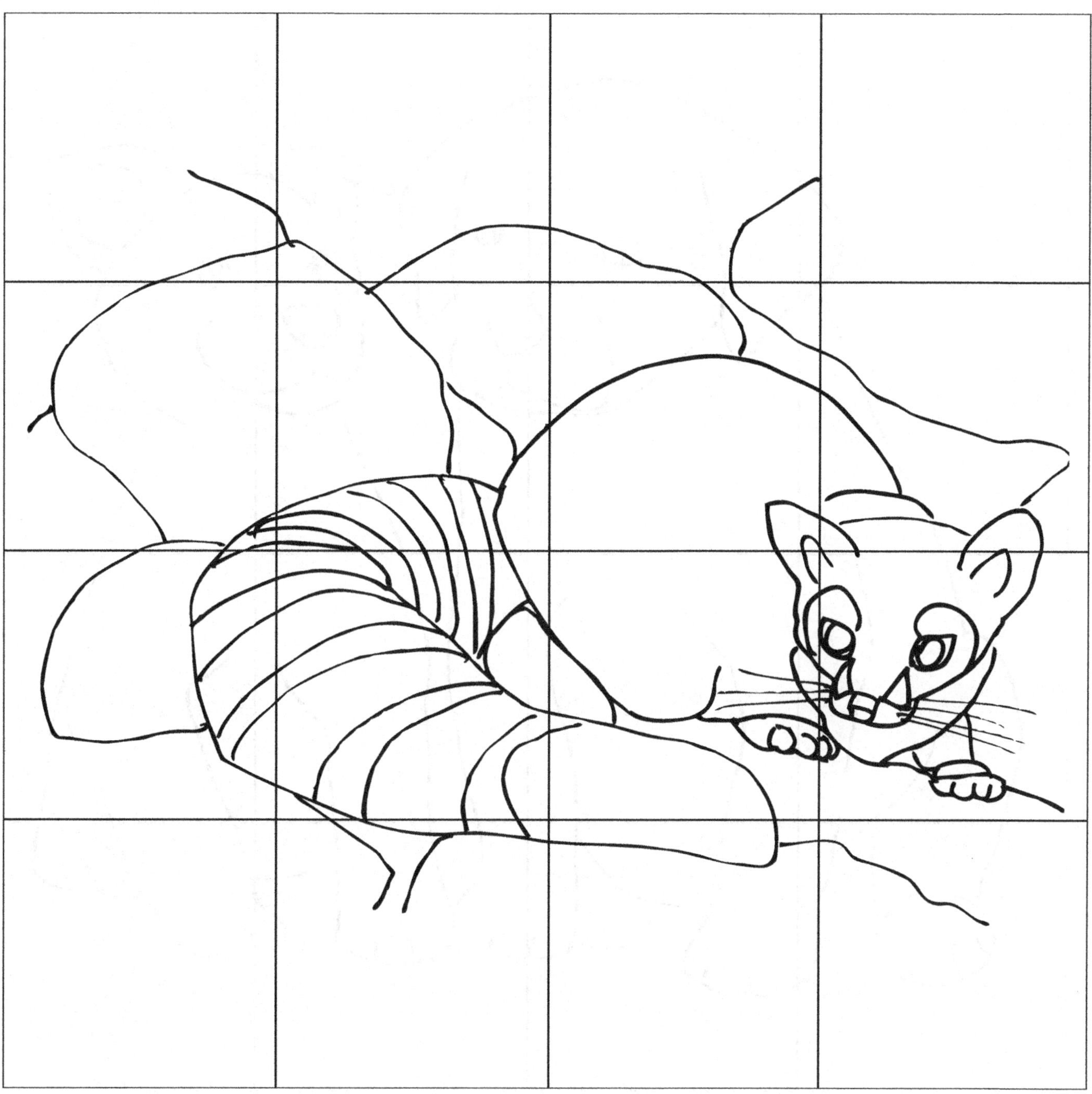

Puppies

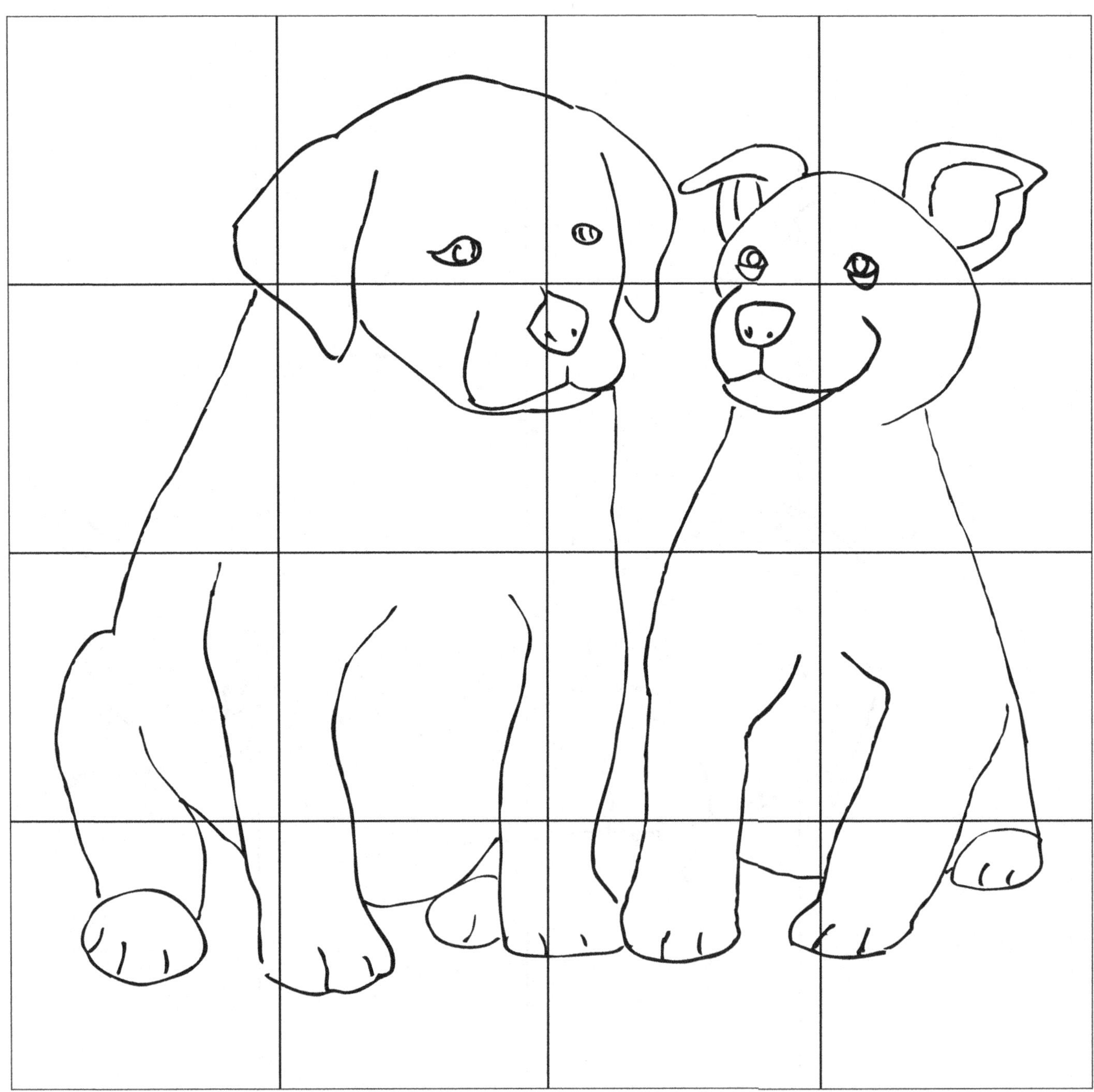

Puppies

Country Road

Country Road

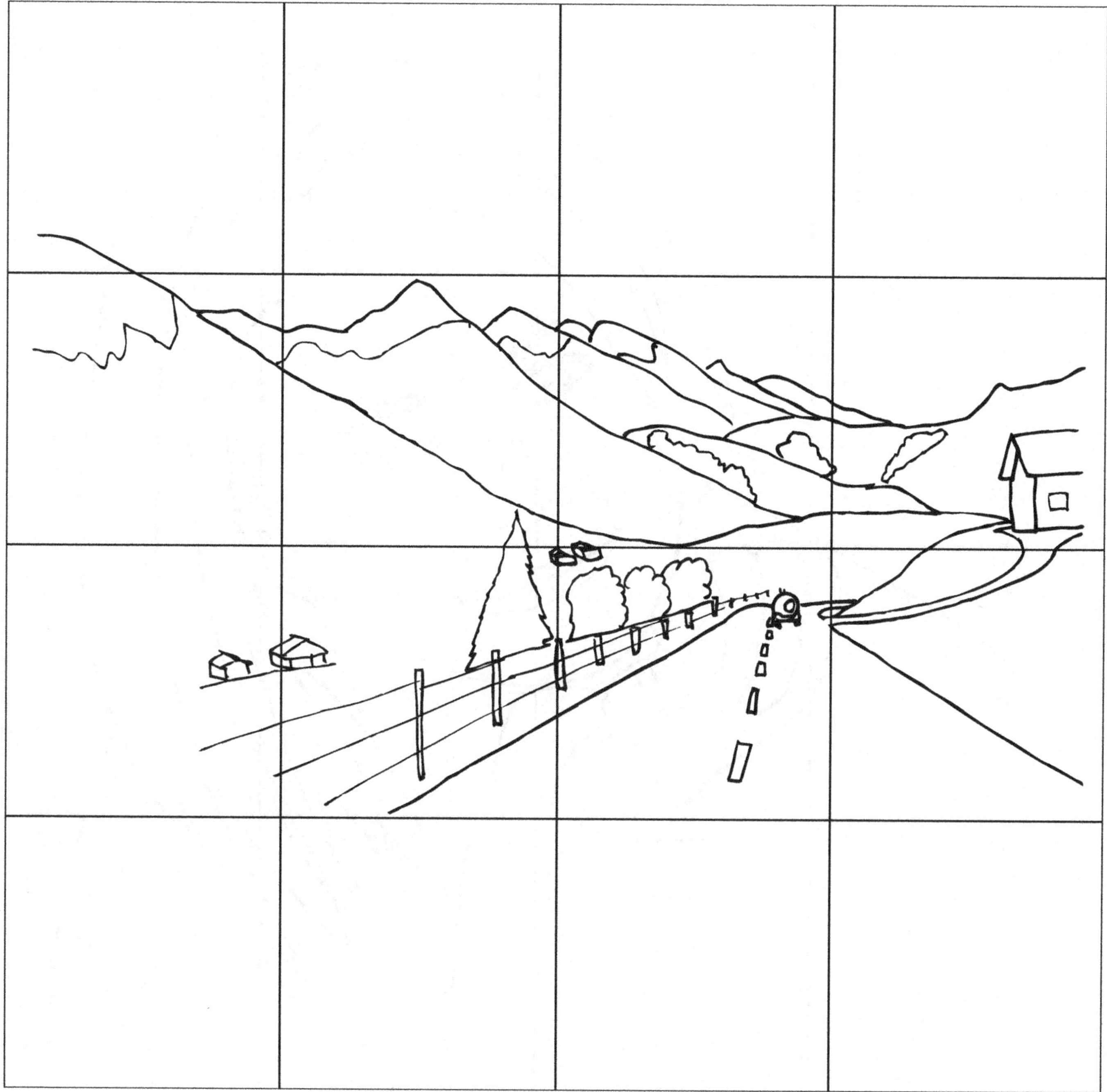

Young Woman

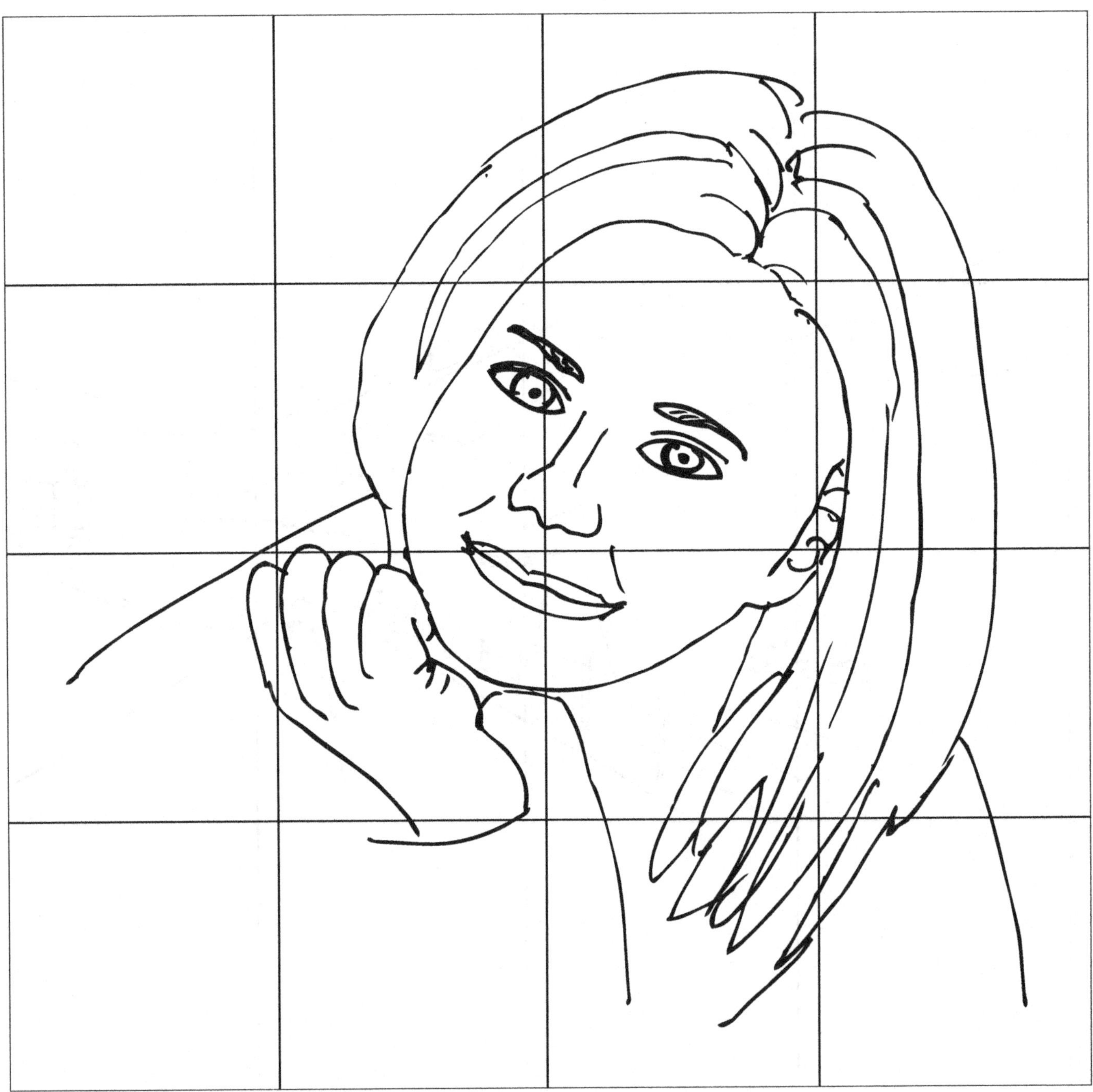

Young Woman

Python

Python

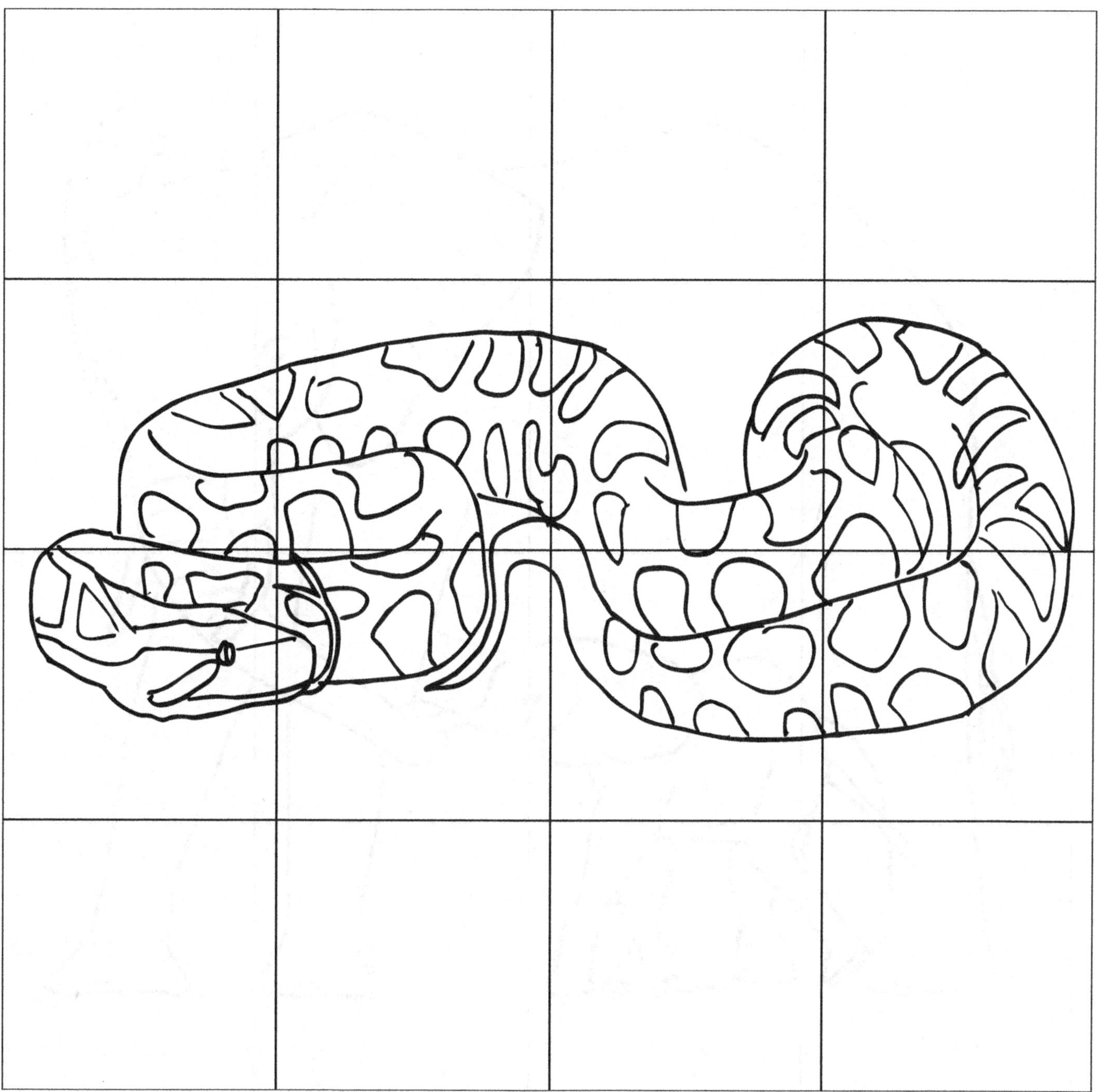

Mother Elephant and Calf

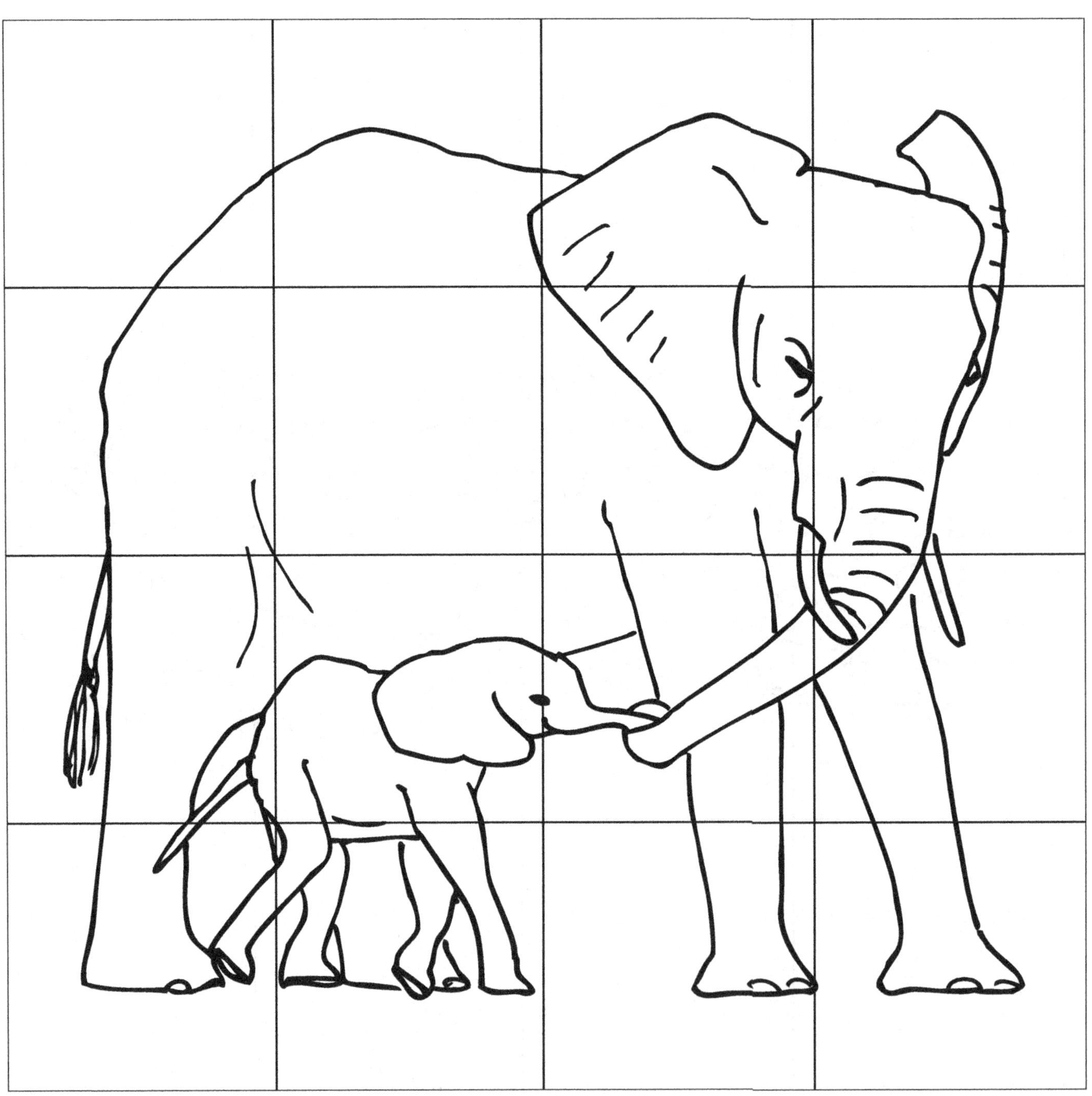

Mother Elephant and Calf

Malayan Tapir and Calf

Malayan Tapir and Calf

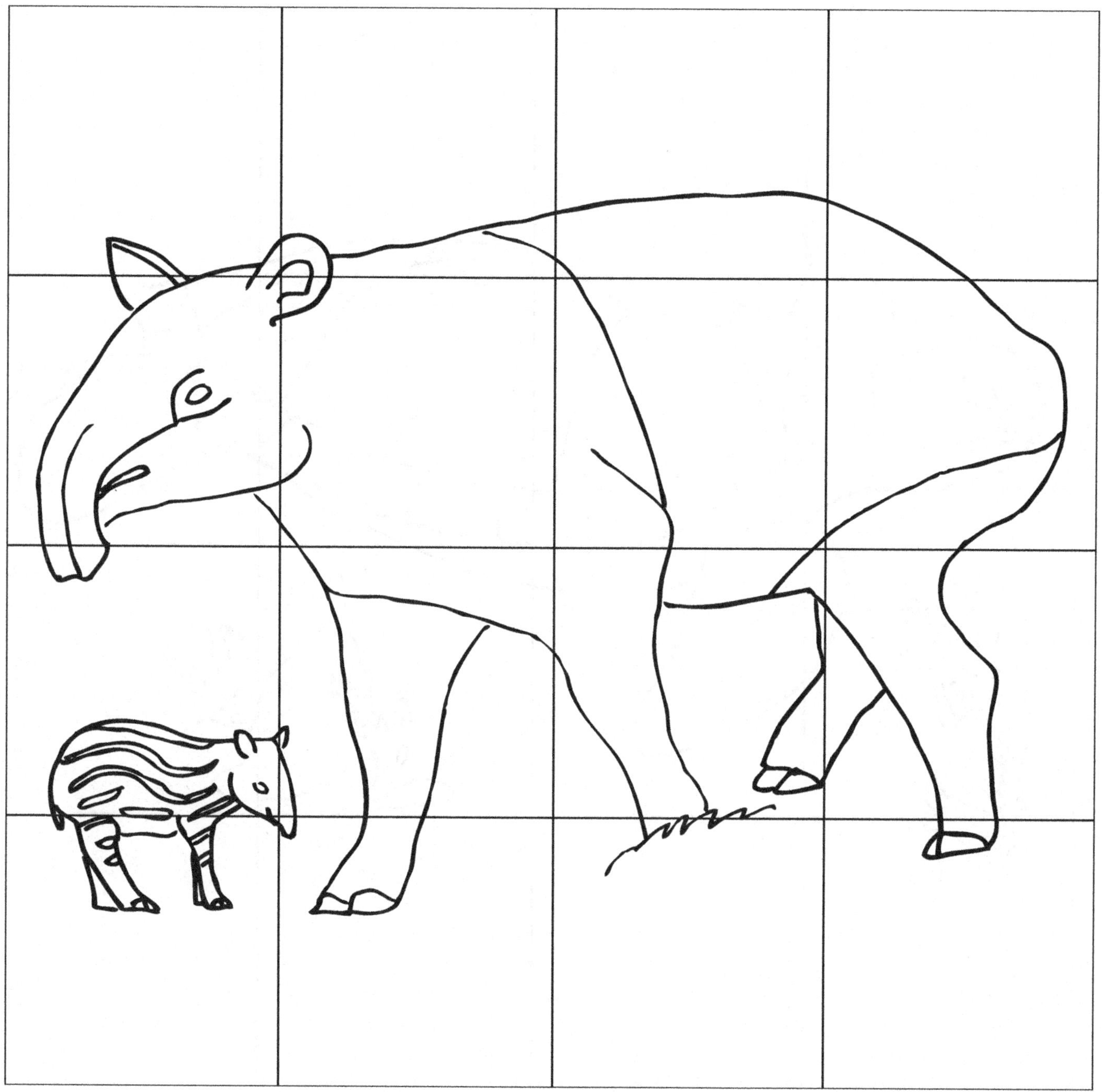

Green Sea Turtle

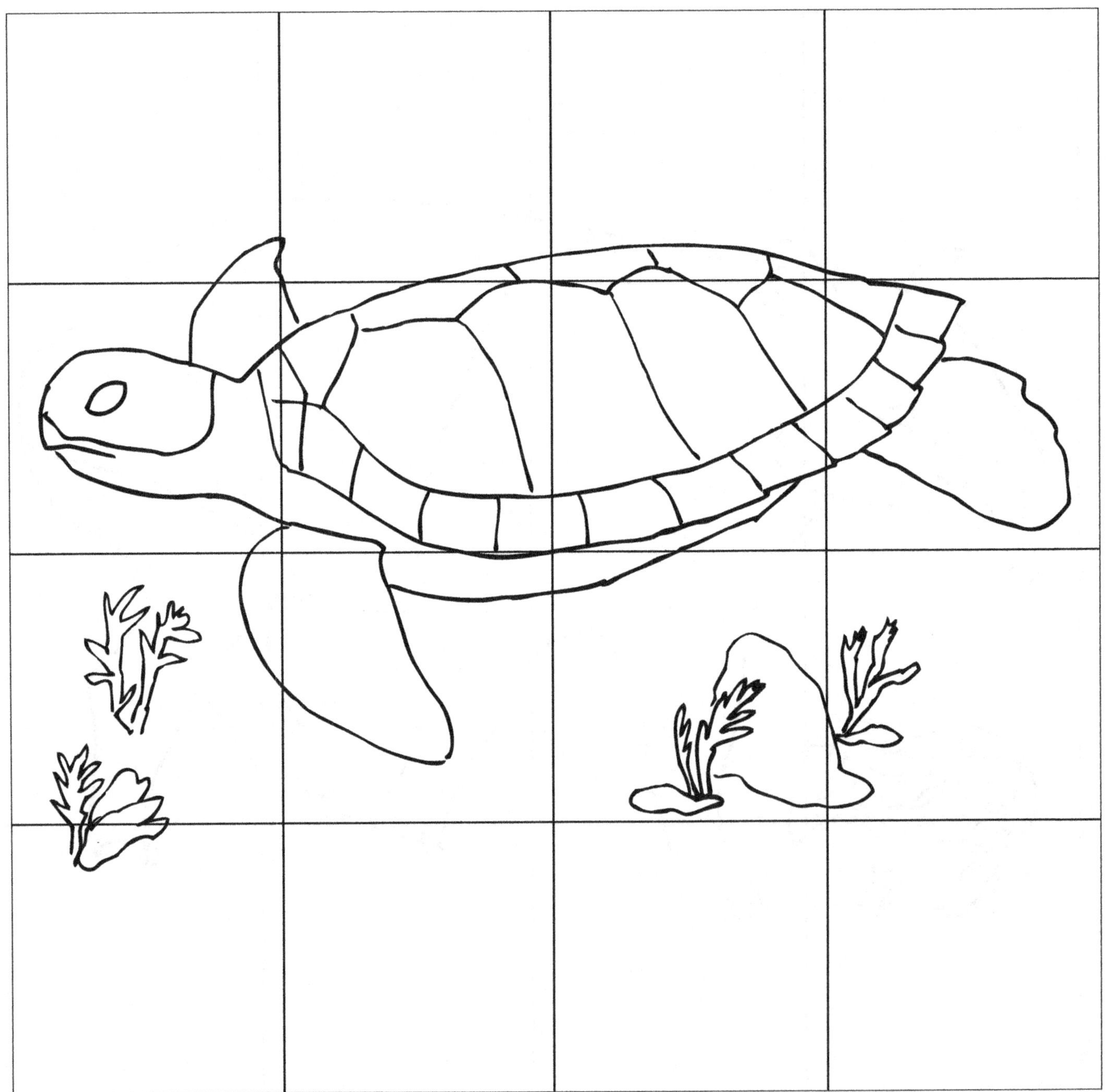

Green Sea Turtle

Whale and Yacht

Whale and Yacht

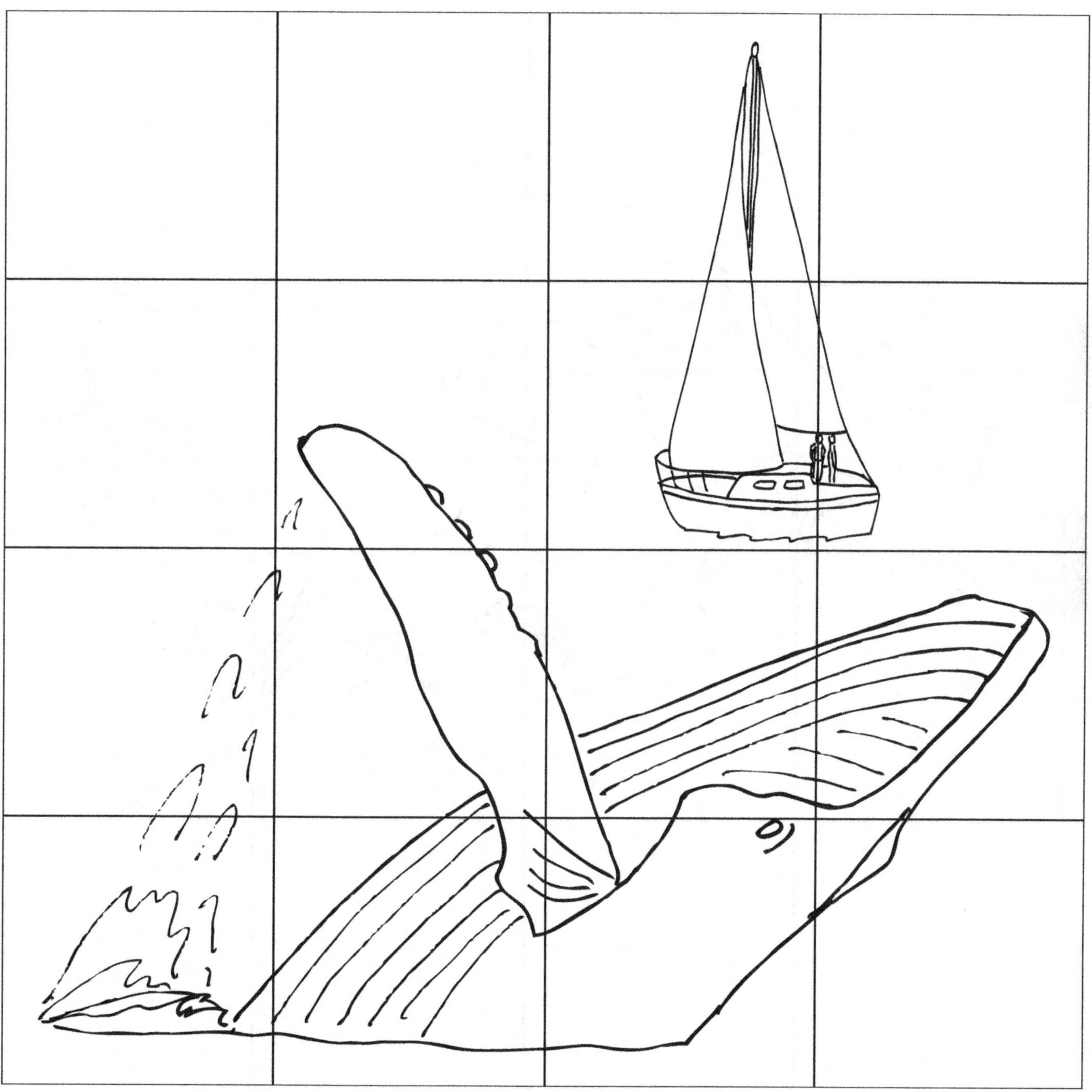

Gouldian Finches

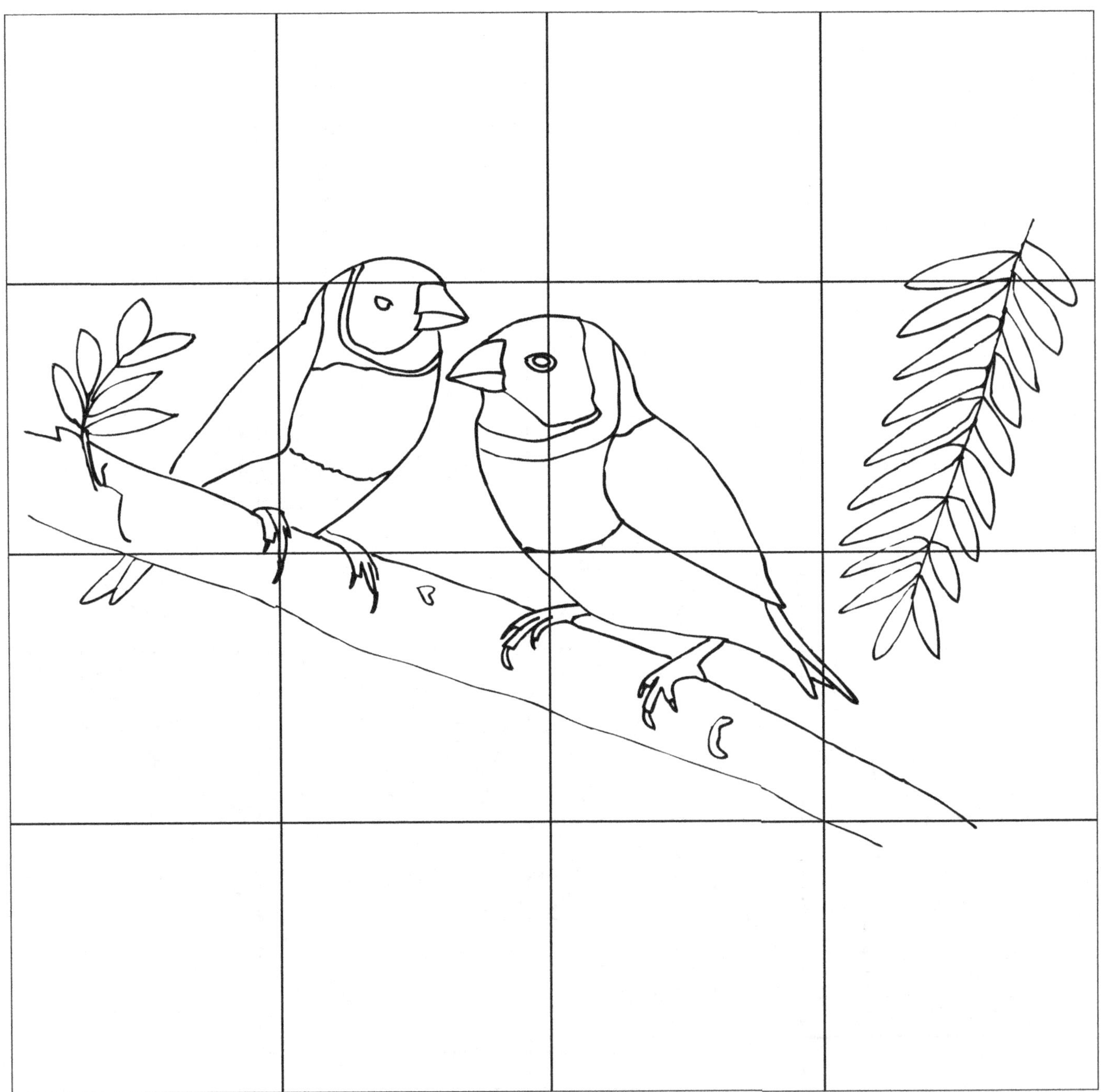

Gouldian Finches

Living Room

Living Room

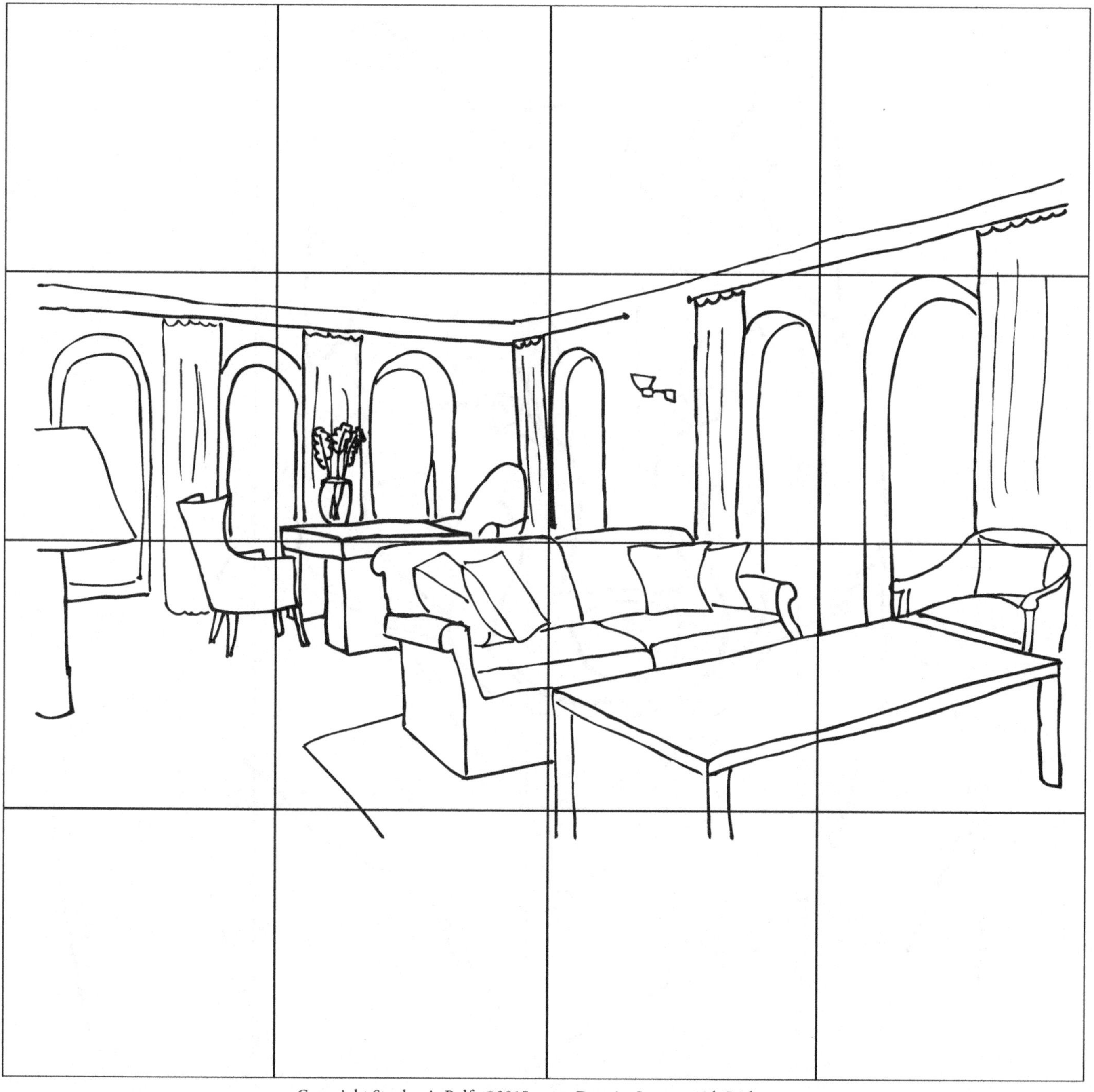

Wolf

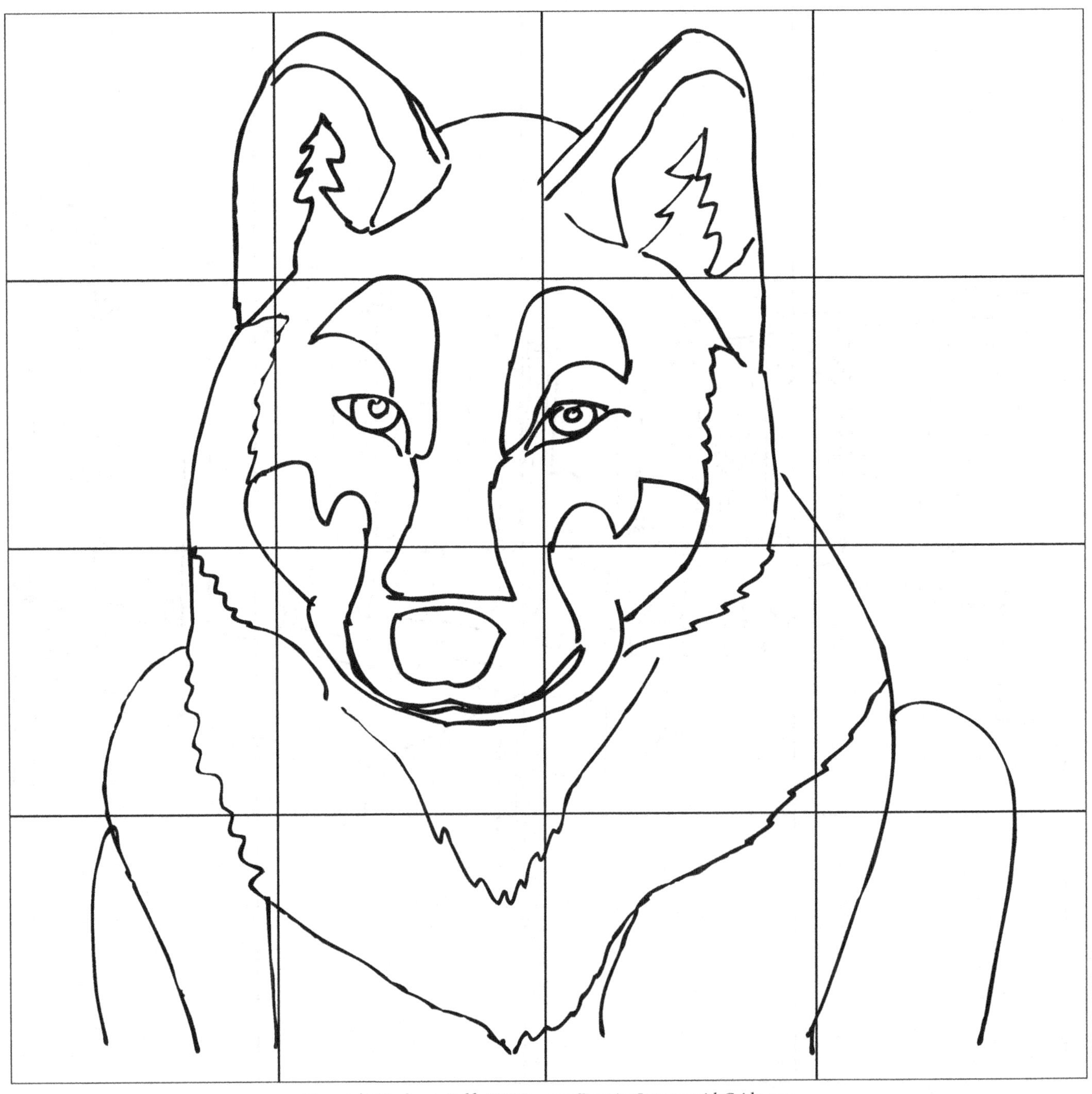

Wolf

Afternoon Walk

Afternoon Walk

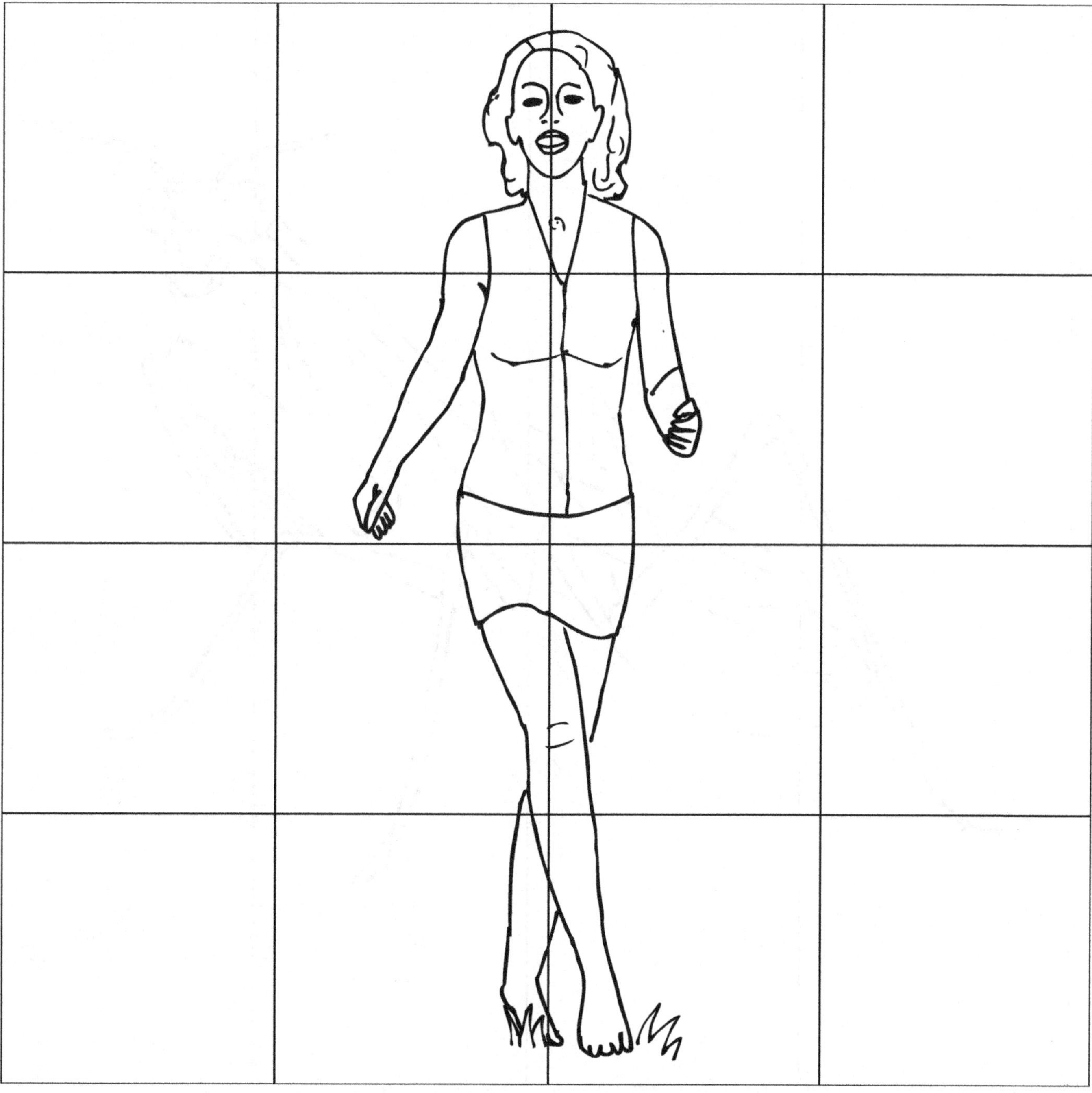

Praying Mantis

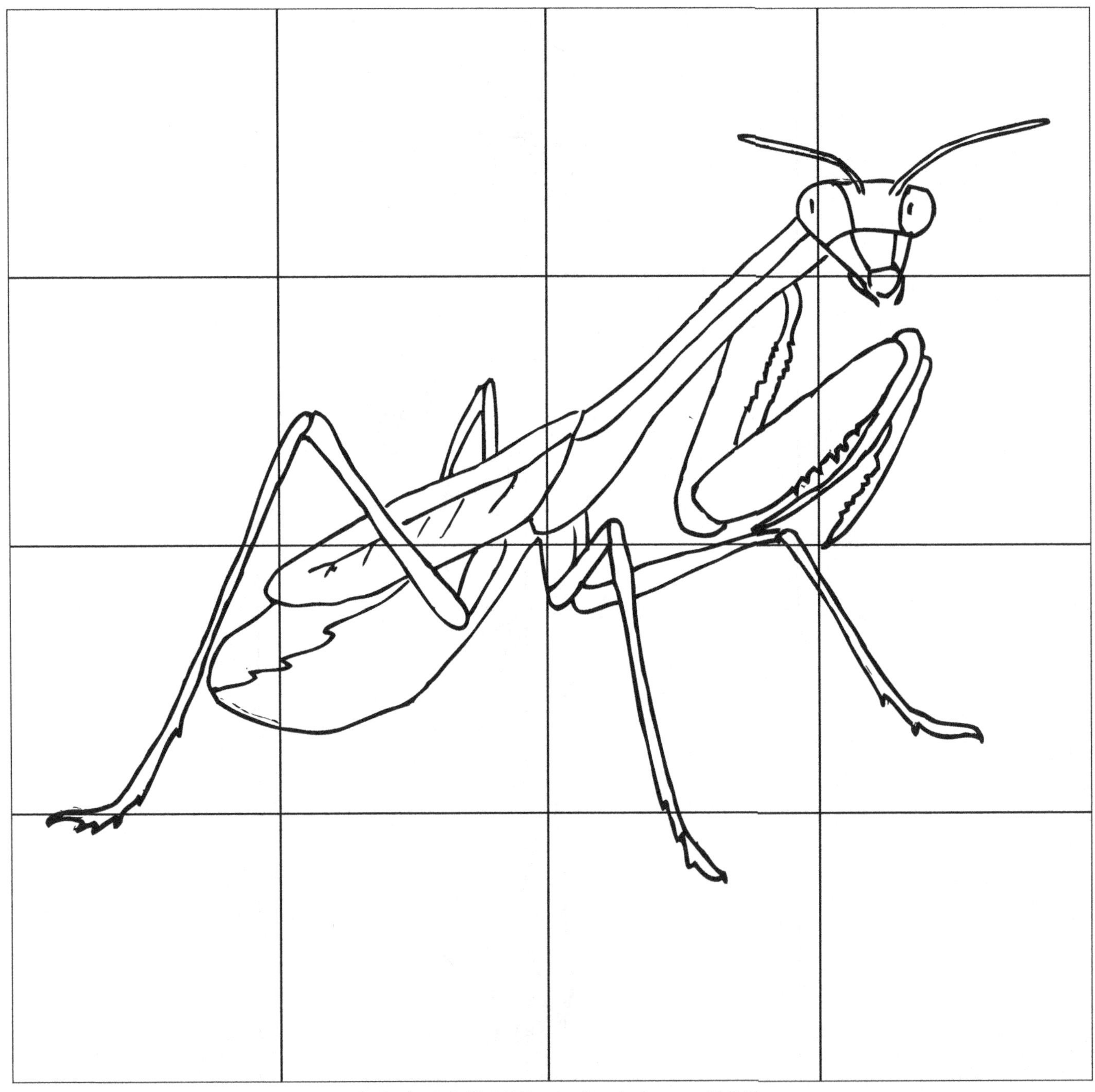

Praying Mantis

Hippopotamus

<table>
<tr><td></td><td></td><td></td><td></td></tr>
<tr><td></td><td></td><td></td><td></td></tr>
<tr><td></td><td></td><td></td><td></td></tr>
<tr><td></td><td></td><td></td><td></td></tr>
</table>

Hippopotamus

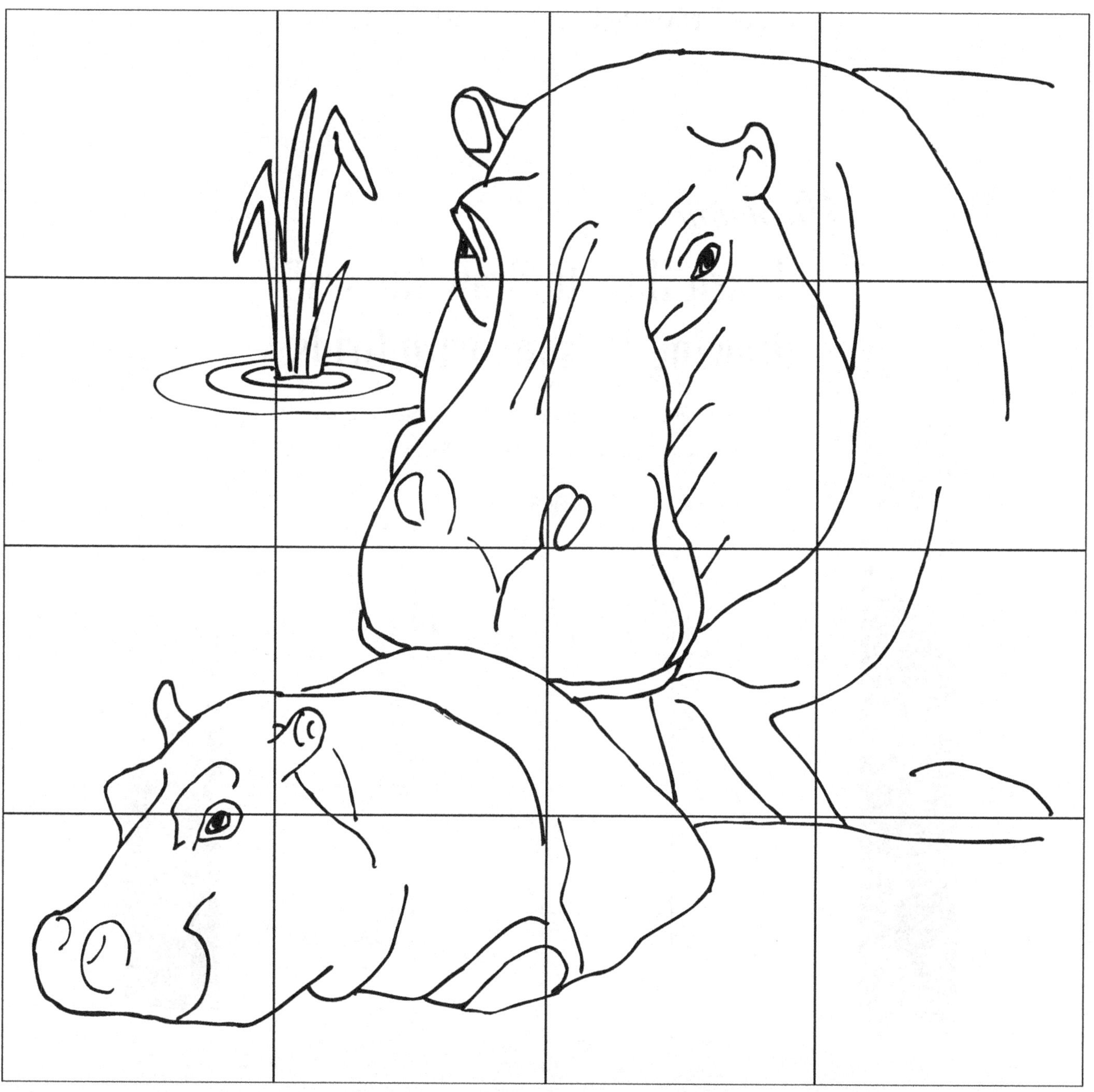

OTHER BOOKS & WEBSITES BY STEPHANIE RELFE

BOOKS

Stephanie's "Learn How to Draw Horses" Drawing Lessons with Grids

Visit the website for new titles:

www.DrawingLessonswithGrids.com

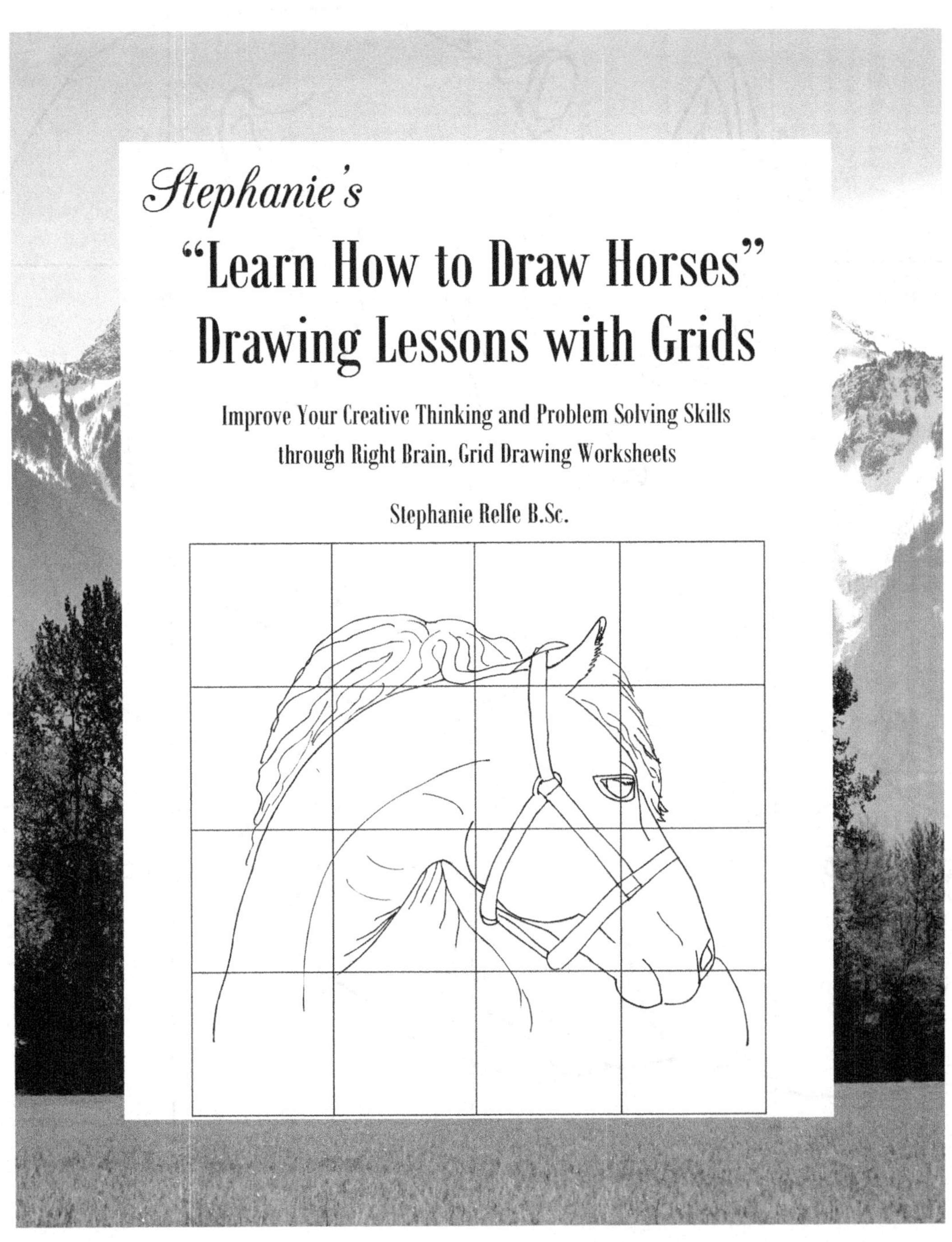

You're not Fat, You're Toxic

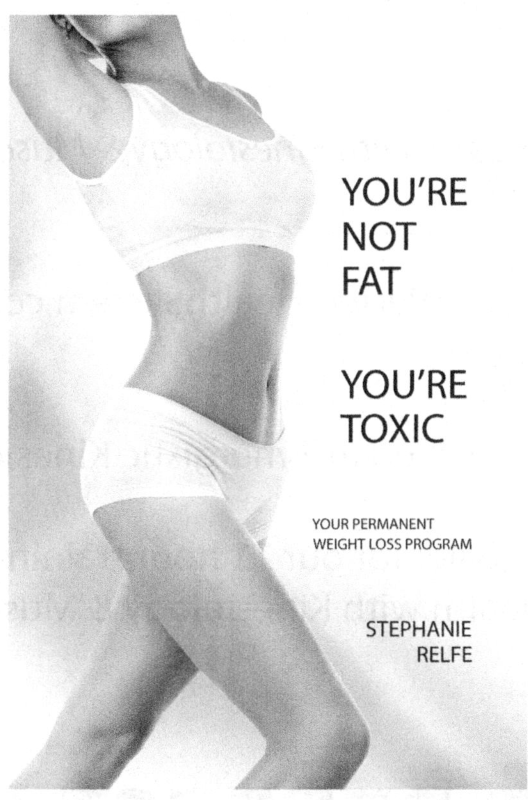

5 Star reviews on Amazon.com.

"This is an awesome book which deserves to be on best seller list as it contains both weight loss and health information not found together in any other single book. It would take you 20 years to track down all this information. Worth every cent. Will truly open your eyes and change your life. Highly recommended."

"I purchased this book about two years ago and have seen some results when sticking to the suggested diets/regiments etc. in this book. As an athlete, and artist (professional ballet dancer) I have had trouble maintaining an appealing weight without taking away from my overall strength versus flexibility, and my body's ability to "keep up". I am an avid fan of natural, preventative medicine, and can appreciate and recognize some of the topics of discussion I have come across while reading this. I will continue to keep this and recommend this book to my fellow dancers. ;-)."

www.YoureNotFatYoureToxic.com

BOOKS & DVD TRAINING SYSTEM

Perfect Health with Kinesiology & Muscle Testing

www.PerfectHealthSystem.com

Get Certified in Synergistic Kinesiology

See the trailer for our 11 hour training system.
Perfect Health with Kinesiology & Muscle Testing

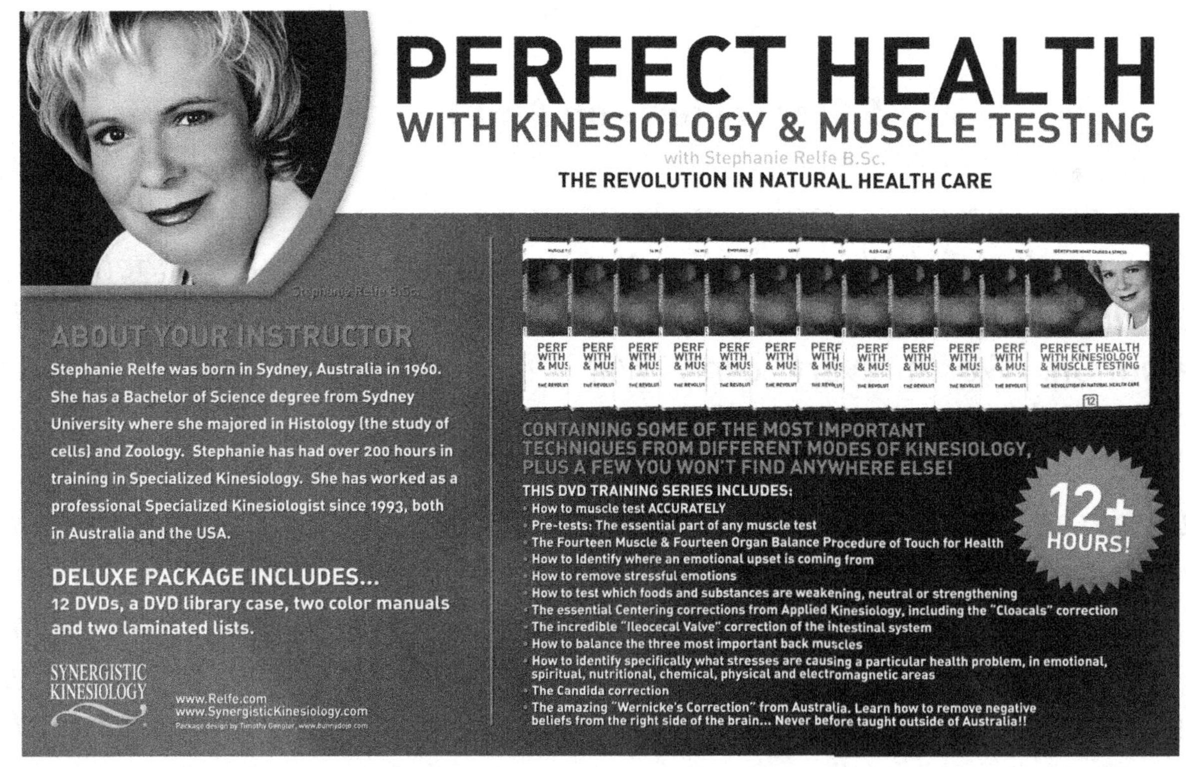

HEALTH, WEALTH & HAPPINESS

www.Relfe.com

"Valuable natural health, mind, spirit, financial and other information unifying the whole, rather than just educating a part of the whole."
Established 1998

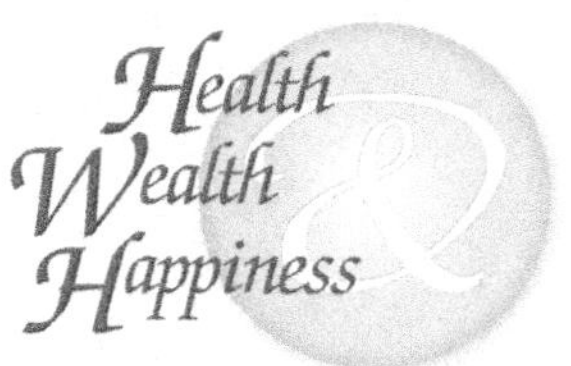

Synergistic Kinesiology

www.SynergisticKinesiology.com

THE KINESIOLOGY REPORT

DIRECT DOWNLOAD - NO SIGNUP

Get this Free Report at www.SynergisticKinesiology.com

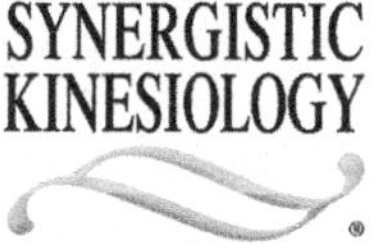